THE
SECOND CRUCIFIXION
OF
NAT
TURNER

THE SECOND CRUCIFIXION OF NAT TURNER

Edited with a new Introduction by
JOHN HENRIK CLARKE

Black Classic Press
Baltimore

THE SECOND CRUCIFIXION OF NAT TURNER

First published 1968
Published 1997 by
Black Classic Press

Introduction copyright 1997 by John Henrik Clarke

Cover Art by Carles Juzang

Library of Congress Catalog Card Number:
96–83452

ISBN: 0–933121–95–4

Printed by **BCP Digital Printing,**
a division of Black Classic Press

Founded in 1978, Black Classic Press specializes in bringing to light obscure and significant works by and about people of African descent. If our books are not available in your area, ask your local bookseller to order them. Our current list can be obtained by visiting our web site at www.blackclassic.com or by writing:

Black Classic Press
·c/o List
P.O. Box 13414
Baltimore, MD 21203

A Young Press With Some Very Old Ideas

DEDICATION

To the memory of William Patterson,
a rebel who always had a cause and a mission
and
To his widow Louise Thompson Patterson,
a friend, colleague, and freedom fighter
who persuaded me to compile and edit this book

INTRODUCTION

In reading the short history of Nat Turner and his revolt in Lerone Bennett's *Pioneers in Protest*, I am reminded of a statement that the late William Patterson often used as a preface to his speeches:

Freedom is a thing you take with your own hands.
It is not willed from one generation to another. If a
generation is fortunate enough to inherit freedom,
they must assume the responsibility of securing it
with their own hands.

The first edition of *William Styron's Nat Turner: Ten Black Writers Respond* was published almost thirty years ago. In my opinion, what the ten Black writers said in response to William Styron's *Confessions of Nat Turner* is even more relevant now. This book is particularly significant for the generation who grew up after the Civil Rights Movement and the Black Studies revolution because the crisis in literature and history concerning the Black man as hero is even more critical now. This subject suffers from naivete and misunderstanding by Black people—naivete and misunderstanding about how power is achieved and used. Nat Turner had an understanding of power in his day superior to any understanding reflected by the Black radicals and revolutionary pretenders of today.

It is not accidental that I have chosen to call the second edition of this book *The Second Crucifixion of Nat Turner*. Nat Turner's first crucifixion was on the gallows in the county of Southampton, Virginia on November 11, 1831 in the town of Jerusalem. Nat Turner's second crucifixion was in the misinterpretation of his life and activity by white writers who chose to play down his rebellion to preclude recognizing him as a genuine radical.

Nat Turner's revolt had a message for his day and a far greater message for our day. That message in part is that no people should ever forget or forgive slavery and humiliation. Nat Turner's revolt was one of the two hundred and fifty slave revolts by Blacks recorded in Herbert Aptheker's ground-breaking book *American Negro Slave Revolts*. In the following excerpt, Aptheker astutely assesses the economic and political circumstances and atmosphere that existed in Virginia when Nat Turner revolted:

> The situation, then in the decade prior to the Southampton revolt is one of extraordinary malaise in the slaveholding area. It is marked by a considerable expansion and development of anti-slavery feeling, nationally and internationally by great and serious unrest among the slave populations in the West Indies as well as on the Continent, by severe economic depression, and by the more rapid growth of the Negro population than the white throughout the old South.
>
> It was into such a situation (one is tempted to assert, though proof is, of course, not at hand, that it was *because* of such a situation) that the upraised dark arms of vengeance of Turner and his followers crashed in the summer of 1831.

In *Pioneers in Protest*, Lerone Bennett is equally penetrating in his analysis of Nat Turner:

> Nat Turner was David Walker's word made flesh. One year after Walker's death and 134 years before Watts, Nat Turner and a band of black rebels cut a swath of blood through the sleepy little Virginia county of Southampton. For forty-eight hours, he and his men hacked and maimed white flesh. When, at length, the insurrection ended, fifty-seven white

persons lay dead and the gaping wound of slavery lay open for all to see. In this effort, the largest and bloodiest slave revolt in American history, Nat Turner made slavery serious. After Nat's insurrection, it was no longer possible for men to pretend. There were men in the slave quarters. One could not always depend on their masks. At any moment, the mask could turn into a horrid face of blood and vengeance.

The story of Nat Turner, however, is as much about the present as it is about the past. Nat Turner was fighting against what the Founding Fathers of this nation said they were against—tyranny! He was fighting for what the Founding Fathers at least implied they were fighting for—Liberty and Justice for All—which ironically did not include Black people in its scope. Even today there is still a concerted effort in the academic community of the Western world not to recognize a Black man as a hero in history. People cannot justify their oppression of others unless they place the object of their oppression outside the pale of humanity, as if God did not create them.

The prototype of twentieth-century revolutionaries, Nat Turner reminds us that oppression is a kind of violence which pays in coins of its own mining. He reminds us that the first and greatest of all gospels is this: that individuals and social systems always reap what they sow.

One cannot understand Nat Turner without understanding the reality that he revealed and then rejected. That reality was American slavery, one of the cruelest social systems designed by human kind. This system was designed to destroy the Black race. The American slave was denied freedom of thought and freedom of movement. The slaves—male and female—belonged body and soul to their master. It was true, literally true, that Black men and women had no rights that white men were bound to respect. In his personal life, Turner experienced one of the glaring contradictions of slavery. Married to a slave woman from another plantation, he had to seek permission from her master to see her. This situation sharpened the tragic circumstance of slavery in his mind. Contrary to the common impression, American slavery was a grimy business that spared neither the master nor the slave. Conflict did not grow out of their situation; conflict was inherent in the situation. That which was human in the slave was always at war with that in the master that breached the bounds of the human.

Nat Turner was a slave–prophet who felt ordained to revolt. Early in his life, Turner saw himself as a person with a mission— a mission to change the condition of slavery or destroy it if the means to do so were ever at his disposal. This mission was part of his total existence. Even while he was growing up, people remarked that he was destined to be more than a slave. In a way, his resolve was a self-proclaimed priesthood. He exercised the kind of discipline on himself that he would later expect of others.

Nat Turner read the same Bible his oppressors read, but he gave it a new interpretation. To Nat Turner, the Bible was revolutionary literature, and he used it accordingly. As a student of the Bible, what he was told about the word of God created such contradictions in Turner's mind that he would ultimately revolt against slavery and all that it stood for. He saw his slave master go to church and pray, so he was told, to a loving and all-forgiving God, who was no respecter of persons, the Father of all, who would dispense His bounty, His kindness, and His mercy equally—on slave master and slave alike. Turner could see that there was something equally ungodly in being a slave master or a slave. He turned to the Bible—the source of his confusion—for and answer. He concluded finally that a strike against slavery was an act of holiness.

Nat Turner is not considered a hero in the general literature of the United States for the same reasons that other great Black rebels, both men and women, have not been given their due in the literature of the world. At one point, the Walt Disney company announced its intention to build a historical theme park in Virginia that would also reflect American slavery. Fortunately, after vigorous protests from the community, plans for the park were scuttled. In my opinion, no such park should be built unless it reflects the kaleidoscope of slavery—runaways, escapees, and slave rebels like Nat Turner. The story would have to include the impressive achievements that African people have made in exile in spite of slavery. Perhaps the greatest achievement of African people away from home is not that they survived but that they also prevailed and went on to produce great literature and music and to build institutions of lasting value.

It has been said that Nat Turner is a hero awaiting an interpreter equal to his heroic place in history. If African people in exile had produced only one Nat Turner, that would have proved Black people were worthy of being free people. There is in the Nat Turner story still another message: African people away from home were in constant revolt. To have survived slavery and all its cruelty removes from Black people forever the stamp of inferiority. What frightens their enemies is that they have transcended simple survival and have proved themselves at critical moments of history when all of the odds were against them. That Black people could move beyond mere survival and teach heroic lessons is indeed frightening to their enemies. The true Nat Turner story says this for the time that he lived in and the message resounds for all time. Nat Turner's story is part of our revolutionary heritage.

—John Henrik Clarke, 1997

CONTENTS

INTRODUCTION

IN A REVIEW OF THE BOOK that is the subject of the essays collected here, the historian Herbert Aptheker has said: "History's potency is mighty. The oppressed need it for identity and inspiration; oppressors for justification, rationalization and legitimacy. Nothing illustrates this more clearly than the history writing on the American Negro people."

The contributors to this book have all addressed themselves to the same subject, each in his own way. The subject: *The Confessions of Nat Turner* by William Styron. No event in recent years has touched and stirred the black intellectual community more than this book. They are of the opinion, with a few notable exceptions, that the Nat Turner created by William Styron has little resemblance to the Virginia slave insurrectionist who is a hero to his people. This being so, then why did William Styron create *his* Nat Turner and ignore the most important historical facts relating to the real Nat Turner? These historical facts are far more dramatic than the imaginary scenes that were created for this novel. Why did William Styron make Nat Turner a celibate with rising lust for what he has called "a pure white belle with swishing skirts"? Why did he ignore the fact that Nat Turner had a wife whom he dearly loved? Thomas Wentworth Higginson, the Colonel of the famous Black Regiment that distinguished itself in the Civil War, in his writings about Nat

Turner, thirty years after the event, established the fact that Nat Turner had a wife—a slave wife on a plantation separate from that of his master. Higginson further points out that the very separation and helplessness of a man to protect his mate was part of the explanation for Nat Turner's revolt against slavery and the plantation system. Great literature is made out of this kind of material. Why did William Styron fail to use it?

The contributors to this book collectively maintain that the distortion of the true character of Nat Turner was deliberate. The motive for this distortion could be William Styron's reaction to the racial climate that has prevailed in the United States in the last fifteen years. Nat Turner, a nineteenth century figure, seems to have been used to make a comment on a twentieth century situation. Why did the character of Nat Turner in Styron's novel vacillate between being a rebel and an uncle tom? Why in spite of his noble calling was he unable to conquer his lust for a white woman? Is there a difference between William Styron's stereotyped portrayal of Nat Turner and the current racial bigots' opinion of civil rights leaders?

In addition to reducing Nat Turner to impotence and implying that Negroes were docile and content with slavery, Styron also dehumanizes every black person in the book. Nat's mother, according to Styron's account, enjoys being raped by a drunken Irish overseer.

In a review in the magazine *Psychology Today* (January 1968) Dr. Lloyd T. Delany warns readers that "These are the confessions of Styron, not Nat Turner, for there exist significant historical discrepancies. . . ." The book's implications about human motivations, he continues, "contain not only serious error, but subtly support certain stereotype views of the most ardent racists."

Why has the book received so much applause from the established press and a large number of well known "scholars" who, in praising this book, display their ignorance of the true story of the Nat Turner revolt? Have they failed to see Nat Turner as a hero and revolutionist out of fear that they might have to see H. Rap Brown and Stokely Carmichael the same way?

The Nat Turner revolt cannot be understood out of context with the atmosphere of revolt that prevailed throughout the first half of the nineteenth century. There were hundreds of uprisings and conspiracies preceding the Southampton, Virginia, uprising led by Nat Turner. The largest of these was the Denmark Vesey conspiracy in Charleston, South Carolina, in 1822. This rebellion was betrayed before it could be put into effect. The startled slaveholders discovered more than 15,000 slaves organized for combat throughout the area. The scene was already set for the Nat Turner revolt.

During the years preceding the Nat Turner revolt there were major uprisings all over the South. The situation in South America and in the Caribbean area was not much different. The slaveholders of Virginia had called for federal troops to support their state militia. In the spring of 1831, federal troops were dispatched to Virginia in time to see service against Nat Turner's rebels. If, as William Styron asserts, the state of Virginia was on the verge of freeing its slaves, why did it assemble so much military might to keep them in bondage?

Thomas Wentworth Higginson, writing in 1861, about the Nat Turner revolt, had this to say:

> It is an unfailing opiate to turn over the drowsy files of the Richmond *Enquirer,* until the moment when these dry and dusty pages are ardently kindled into flame by the torch of Nat Turner. Then the terror flared on, increasing, until the remotest Southern States were found shuddering at nightly rumors of insurrection; until far off European colonies—Antigua, Martinique, Caraccas, Tartola—recognized by some secret sympathy the same epidemic alarms; until the very boldest words of freedom were reported as uttered in the Virginia House of Delegates with unclosed

doors; until an obscure young man named Garrison was indicted at common law in North Carolina, and had a price set upon his head by the Legislature of Georgia. . . . Thus, for instance, we know that Nat Turner's young wife was a slave; we know that she belonged to a different master from himself; we know little more than this, but this is much. For this is equivalent to saying that, by day or by night, her husband had no more power to protect her than the man who lies bound upon a plundered vessel's deck has power to protect his wife on board the pirate schooner disappearing in the horizon.

It should not now be necessary to search for the motives, personal and otherwise, for the Nat Turner revolt. The documents relating to this revolt and slave insurrections in general are numerous. One of the many that I found to be particularly useful is: "An Account of Some of the Principal Slave Insurrections, Collected From Various Sources," by Joshua Coffin. Published in New York in 1860 by the American Anti-Slavery Society.

In his essay Lerone Bennett has said that Nat Turner still awaits a literary interpreter worthy of his sacrifice. The other contributors to this book make the same point, in different ways. In all insurrections, the standing wonder seems to be that the slaves most trusted and best used should be most deeply involved. So in the Nat Turner case, as usual, men resorted to the most astonishing theories about the origin of the uprising. And our Nat is still waiting.

—JOHN HENRIK CLARKE
March 1968

CHAPTER I

NAT'S LAST WHITE MAN

LERONE BENNETT, JR.

History takes still more from those who have lost everything, and gives yet more to those who have taken everything. For its sweeping judgments acquit the unjust and dismiss the pleas of their victims. History never confesses.

                                              —MAURICE MERLEAU-PONTY

THERE ARE EIGHT MEMORABLE LINES in the *Confessions* of William Styron.

These lines, which are worthy of a better setting, illuminate a scene of great power and perception.

Nat Turner, his deed done, is sitting in a prison cell regarding Thomas Gray, a treacherous and unctuously condescending white man who is trying to worm his way into the black psyche for purposes of white aggrandizement. Nat regards this specimen with distaste and repulsion. He knows why Gray is there. He knows that Gray is working with the enemy, and he begins to wonder about the experiences which produce such men. Of a sudden, Styron writes, Nat has an "impression, dim and fleeting, of hallucination, of talk buried deep in dreams." He stares long and hard at Gray and perceives that he is "little different from any of the others," adding: ". . . nonetheless it was a matter of wonder to me where this my last white man (save one with the rope) had come from. Now, as many times before, I had the feeling I had made him up. It was impossible to talk to an invention, therefore I remained all the more determinedly silent."

Nat Turner speaks these lines on page 35 and then disappears from William Styron's *Confessions,* having warned the reader that he continues at his own risk. What is truly remarkable is that William Styron could write these lines without realizing that he was judging himself as well as Thomas Gray. For Styron has, in fact, replaced Thomas Gray, the author of the first *Confessions,* as Nat Turner's Last White Man. And the *Confessions* of William Styron proves that it is still impossible to talk to white inventions.

Except for the lines indicated and a few random quotes from the original *Confessions,* Nat Turner does not speak in William Styron's *Confessions.*

The voice in this confession is the voice of William Styron.

The images are the images of William Styron.

The confession is the confession of William Styron.

And Styron's *Confessions,* despite the revealing hosannas of the white culture structure, is a record of the hallucinatory silence of our history, of 350 years "of talk buried deep in dreams." Styron *dreams,* but he refuses to confront history and that refusal defines his book which tells us little about the historical Nat Turner and a great deal about William Styron and the white culture structure which made the book a modern literary happening.

Styron tells us he is meditating on history. But we are not fooled. We know that he is really trying to escape history. We know—he confesses it—that he is trying to escape the judgment of history embodied in Nat Turner and his spiritual sons of the twentieth century.

Styron begins his flight from Nat Turner—and history—by substituting a white panoply of fantasies for the historical girders of the Nat Turner cataclysm.[1] Instead of following

[1] The basic historical document is *The Confessions of Nat Turner,* Thomas R. Gray, Baltimore, 1831. This "confession" was prepared by a white man hostile to Nat Turner and the cause he represented. Some lines in the Gray *Confessions* are obviously spurious. (Nat prob-

the traditional technique of the historical novelist, who works within the tension of accepted facts, Styron forces history to move within the narrow grooves of his preconceived ideas.

According to the historical data, the real Nat Turner was a virile, commanding, courageous figure. Styron rejects history by rejecting this image of Nat Turner. In fact, he wages literary war on this image, substituting an impotent, cowardly, irresolute creature of his own imagination for the real black man who killed or ordered killed real white people for real historical reasons. The man Styron substitutes for Nat Turner is not only the antithesis of Nat Turner; he is the antithesis of blackness. In fact, he is a standard Styron type: a neurasthenic, Hamlet-like white intellectual in blackface.

We are not quibbling here over footnotes in scholarly journals. We are objecting to something more insidious, more dangerous. *We are objecting to a deliberate attempt to steal the meaning of a man's life.* And that attempt must be condemned in the name of the man whose name has been illicitly appropriated for a dubious literary adventure.

One wonders really why William Styron entitled his book *The Confessions of Nat Turner* instead of *The Confessions of Samuel Washington* or *The Confessions of William Styron.*

---

ably did not say that "we found no more victims to gratify our thirst for blood.") It is also probable that Gray suppressed some facts and gave undue emphasis to others. But, for all its limitations, the Gray *Confessions* remains the primary document. And it contains lines which are obviously genuine, particularly the passages in which Nat describes his visions. Thomas Gray was hardly up to inventions of that order. It should also be noted that Nat Turner was served better in many instances by Thomas Gray, the avowed racist, than by William Styron, the avowed liberal. In addition to the Gray document, there is a rich tradition surrounding the event and some references in contemporary newspapers. See also W. S. Drewry, *Slave Insurrections in Virginia, 1830–1865,* Washington, 1900; Robert Howinson, *History of Virginia,* Philadelphia, 1846–48; Herbert Aptheker, *American Negro Slave Revolts,* New York, 1943.

For it is obvious on the face of it that Styron has little interest in deepening our understanding of Nat Turner. On the contrary, it seems, to this reader anyway, that Styron is *using* Nat Turner as a counter in two desperate and rather pathetic private games.

In the first game, Styron is writing for his very life, throwing up smokescreen after smokescreen to hide himself from the truth of the American experience. On this level, it is the thrust of his art to reconcile Nat Turner to an unacceptable reality by making him confess that he would have spared at least one white person.[2] ("Go ye into the city and find one . . . just one.") In this desperate game, Styron uses the white woman as bait, tempting his central character with page after page of squirming white buttocks, "bare white full round hips" and "milky white legs and arms." By this method, Styron shifts the focus of the Turner insurrection, downgrading the main issues (white oppression and black liberation) and elevating the white woman to a position of central importance. The child-woman, Margaret, who was a victim of history, becomes the central image by which Styron rejects history. It is she who turns Nat from hatred of his own people to a missionary effort of uplift.[3] It is she who brings Nat to partial repentance. It is she whom Nat

[2] In fact, Nat Turner did spare one family of poor whites. See Governor John Floyd's statement in Aptheker, *American Negro Slave Revolts, op. cit.* But this was an act of social criticism and it is social criticism—and history—Styron is fleeing. It is the burden of his art to reduce the social to the personal, to reduce institutionalized oppression to isolated acts of personal outrage, to reduce history to sex.

[3] In an incredible scene, Styron's Nat turns with loathing from black people. "My eyes," he said, "search the white crowd, finally discover Margaret Whitehead, her dimpled chin tilted up as, with one arm entwined in her mother's, she carols heavenward, a radiance like daybreak on her serene young face. Then, slowly and softly, like a gentle outrush of breath, my hatred of the Negroes diminishes, dies, replaced by a kind of wild, desperate love for them, and my eyes are wet with tears." Styron, *Confessions*, p. 104.

visions as he mounts the gallows. Never before, it seems to me, has the white woman been used with such cynicism and desperation.

On another level, Styron is playing the "new history" game of reviving Big Black Sambo. In other words, he is trying to prove that U. B. Phillips, the classic apologist for slavery, and Stanley Elkins, the sophisticated modern apologist, were right when they projected Sambo—the bootlicking, head-scratching child-man—as a dominant plantation type. The suggestion here is that the Afro-American slave went beyond the call of the whip in accommodating himself to slavery, that slavery, as Styron says, "dehumanized the slave and divested him of honor, moral responsibility and manhood" and that "the character (not characterization) of 'Sambo' . . . did in fact exist."[4]

Styron *knows* that Sambo existed. What he does not know —because he does not *know* himself—is that antebellum southerners and their modern descendants had to believe that Sambo existed in order to deal with the contradictions of their own existence.

Styron proves this inadvertently. For we catch him red-handed manipulating evidence in order to make Nat Turner and his aides—the very antithesis of the Sambo myth—confirmers of the Elkins-Phillips-Styron dream. In fact, Styron is so determined to prove that his dream exists that he gives his main character the mind and vocabulary of U. B. Phillips. And he performs the amazing feat of actually putting the Sambo thesis in Nat Turner's mouth. On pages 55 and 56, Nat is filled with rage by the "harmless, dull, malleable docility" of Hark and he discourses in the best "new history" mode on "the unspeakable bootlicking Sambo, all giggles and smirks and oily, sniveling servility."

Styron accomplishes this literary sleight of hand by sup-

[4] See Styron's review of *American Negro Slave Revolts* in *The New York Review of Books,* September 26, 1963.

pressing facts and inventing "facts." Since he has already
admitted that he departed "from cut-and-dried facts,"[5] I will
only say here that there is a pattern in his distortion of the
facts and that the pattern is meaningful.

First of all, and most important of all, there is a pattern
of emasculation which mirrors America's ancient and manic
pattern of de-balling black men. There is a second pattern,
which again mirrors the white man's praxis, a pattern of de-
structuring the black family and the black group. And these
patterns contribute to an overall pattern of destruction in
which the historical Nat Turner is deracinated and made
impotent and irrelevant.

Consider, for example, Styron's assault on Nat Turner's
family.

Nat tells us in the Gray *Confessions* that he grew up in a
strong family unit which buttressed his sense of identity and
mission. He speaks with fondness of his father and mother
who taught him to read and write. He also remembers his
grandmother who was, he says, "very religious, and to whom
I was much attached. . . ."

William Styron disapproves of the historical arrangements
of the Turner family. He *knows* the Turner family. In other
words, he has an idea of the black family which contradicts
Nat Turner's reality, and he begins his book by making Nat
Turner's reality conform to his idea. Nat's beloved grandmother is immediately banished. "I never laid eyes on my
grandmother," Styron's Nat says. Nat is also denied the support of his father, who fled to the North after instilling a
burning sense of mission in his son. In Gray's *Confessions*,
Nat says that when he was three or four he was told that
he "surely would be a prophet," adding: "*And my father and
mother* strengthened me in this my first impression, saying
in my presence, I was intended for some great purpose . . ."
[Emphasis added]. That same line appears in Styron's *Confessions* in a remarkably revealing translation. Styron's Nat

[5] *The New York Times,* February 11, 1968.

says, *"And my mother* strengthened me in this my first impression, . . ." [Emphasis added]. Styron has eliminated the troublesome black father.

Having created a proper ADC slave family, Styron works his white magic on Turner's mother. According to tradition, Nat's mother was an African native who hated slavery so much that she was determined not to add to the slave population. At Nat's birth, she was so enraged that she had to be tied to keep her from murdering Nat. This passion for freedom was unfortunate from Styron's viewpoint. For he wanted Nat to be a "house nigger" and the son of a "house nigger." He therefore pushed this incident back a generation. In his book, Nat's *grandmother* is enraged at the birth of Nat's mother.

By this alchemy, Styron detaches mother and son from black people. And mother and son become burlesques of the traditional "house nigger" types. Nat's mother, for example, is always reminding Nat of his special place in the plantation pecking order. "Us folks in de house," she says, "is *quality!*" Styron forces this viewpoint (his viewpoint) on his central character who feels toward his old marsa a "feeling one should bear only toward the divinity." A pet, "the little black jewel of Turner's Mill," he is taught to read in Styron's fantasy not by his father and mother but by the good white folks.

Styron pursues his fantasy by filling his main character with immense loathing for black people. The man erroneously and libelously identified as Nat Turner begins "more and more to regard the Negroes of the mill and field as creatures beneath contempt," as "a lower order of people, a ragtag mob, coarse, raucous, clownish, uncouth." He identifies black people with animals and he is made to say (by Styron) that "my black shit-eating people were surely like flies, God's mindless outcasts, lacking even that will to destroy by their own hands their unending anguish." The converse of this hatred for blackness is reverence for whiteness. Styron's character has a fantasy about possessing the plantation and says: "In a twinkling I became white—white as clabber cheese, white, stark white, white as a Marble Episcopalian. . . . I was no longer the grinning black boy in velvet pantaloons; for a fleeting moment instead I owned all, and so exercised the privilege of ownership by unlacing my fly and pissing loudly on the same worn stone where dainty tiptoeing feet had gained the veranda steps a short three years before. What a strange, demented ecstasy! How white I was! What wicked joy!"

What a strange, demented fantasy!

Even stranger is the fact that Styron apparently believes in the smokescreens of his own mind. Relentlessly, remorselessly, he pursues his cardboard Nat Turner, stuffing his mind with U. B. Phillips platitudes. Styron's Nat sees himself in the mirror, "eyes rolling white with nervous vigilance." He sees a black man in the distance "groping in vain for the source of some intolerable itch." He sees black people in church "mouths agape or with sloppy uncomprehending smiles, shuffling their feet. Suddenly they seem to me as meaningless and as stupid as a barn full of mules, and I hate them one and all." He observes a group of slaves who have been sold South and he is "haunted and perplexed by the docile equanimity and good cheer with which these simple black people, irrevocably uprooted, would set out to encounter a strange and unknown destiny." The poor dumb creatures didn't seem to care. Parting "from a place which had been their entire universe for years caused them no more regret than did the future cast over them worry or foreboding." They were children, hopeless children, twittering and giggling. They were, Styron's Nat thinks, "like animals" and they "deserved to be sold."

As for freedom, Styron's Nat has doubts about it. Mouthing the classic apology of antebellum southerners, the character bearing the name of one of the most passionate rebels in American history says it is useless to free such creatures.

"For what," he asks, "could freedom mean to Arnold?"
Is this the voice of Nat Turner?
Of course not. William Styron is *playing*. He is trying to
hide the real Nat Turner.
The real Nat Turner was one with his destiny. He was one
with his people. He recalls in the original *Confessions* that
he grew "up among them" and that "such was the confidence
of the Negroes in the neighborhood, even at this early period
of my life, in my superior judgment, that they would often
carry me with them when they were going on any roguery,
to plan for them."

This Nat Turner is displaced in the book by the white
man in blackface who settles down into the "silent, cease-
lessly vigilant, racking solitude" Styron has prepared for him.

What is this if not a project of destruction involving the
vitals of the historical personage named Nat Turner?

Styron carries this project to its ultimate end by emasculating Nat Turner. In the process, he ignores evidence which
indicates that Nat had a slave wife. According to Thomas
Wentworth Higginson, contemporary newspapers reports
said Nat's wife "was tortured under the lash, after her husband's execution, to make her produce his papers. . . ."[6]
Higginson's report is supported by the oral tradition. W. S.
Drewry reports that "Nat's son, Redic, survived him."

But this evidence clashes with Styron's purposes. So, he
consummates the white fantasy by defusing Nat sexually. In
Styron's fantasy, Nat Turner becomes an impotent, sex-
crazed celibate who masturbates every Saturday in the car-
penter's shop. And it is *always* "a nameless white girl
between whose legs" he envisions himself—"a young girl with
golden curls."

Styron also provides his character with a homosexual encounter and a detailed white fantasy life. From first to last,
the white man masquerading as Nat Turner is slavering over

[6] Thomas Wentworth Higginson, *Travellers and Outlaws*, Boston,
1889.

some childish southern belle. There is "Miss Emmeline" with her "lustrous rich auburn hair" and her "fair and slender fingers." There is the fiancée of Major Ridley with her "soft white thighs" and a neck as "white as a water lily." There is, above all else, Margaret Whitehead with her "fine white skin, milky, transparent" and her hands "white as milk glass, blue-veined." Not only that: Styron's character is so attuned to whiteness that a white voice turns him on. Languishing in prison, he hears "the voice of a young girl singing. Sweet and gentle, from some white, delicate throat. . . ."

Condemned by silence and by emphasis is black flesh. Styron's character has only one fantasy of a black woman and she is—you guessed it—a whore—"a plump doxy, every nigger boy's Saturday piece. . . ." But the black woman fails to excite him and he fastens in his mind on a young white woman, "some slippery-tongued brown-headed missy with a sugar-sweet incandescent belly who as I entered her cried out with pain and joy and enveloped me convulsively with milky-white legs and arms. . . ."

Now, obviously, someone has an enormous white-woman problem. But since there is not one shred of evidence to indicate that Nat Turner was obsessed by the traditional obsession of the white male, we can only wonder why William Styron dreams of black revolutionaries dreaming of white thighs.

Nat Turner tells us in the original *Confessions* that *he* was obsessed by black liberation. And he tells us that he spent most of his life preparing for his great mission. Styron does not introduce us to *that* black revolutionary. Inexplicably, he omits the fact that Nat ran away from his master. And he refuses to confront the man who talked to God and who heard God order the destruction of the enemies of God and man. *That* man, I say, is not in William Styron's book. Also absent is the man who refused to plead guilty at his trial, "saying to his counsel, that he did not feel so."

It should also be said that William Styron shows no

understanding of the psychology which makes slaves rise up and cut their oppressors' throats from ear to ear. Styron evades this dynamic; he refuses to come to grips with the institutionalized violence of an oppressive status quo and the inevitable counter violence of the oppressed.

Instead of dealing seriously with these questions, Styron continues his game of evasion by inventing a power struggle between Nat and Will and by weighing Nat down with white complexes. Nat, in Styron's fantasy, fears and loathes his aide, Will, who is described as a mad animal, "a wild boar hog." According to Styron, Will, who wants to "get some of dat white stuff," forces his way into the rebellion. This contradicts the facts as established by the Gray *Confessions*. In that document, Nat says he arrived at the rendezvous spot and found two new recruits, Will and Jack. "I saluted them on coming up," he says, "and asked Will how came he there, he answered, his life was worth no more than others, and his liberty as dear to him. I asked him if he thought to obtain it? He said he would, or lose his life. That was enough to put him in full confidence." In his determination to reduce liberty to personal passions and history to "some of dat white stuff," Styron ignores this evidence and questions Nat Turner's credentials as a leader. At the moment of truth, Nat is presented as a panicky, fearful, impotent man, "retching in the bushes" at the sight of blood. Nearly "torn apart by frights and apprehensions," he is unable to strike a death blow and he condemns his "womanish failure to strike down white flesh."

Styron's fantasy also contradicts the psychology of the black rebel who told a racist in Virginia in 1831: "I placed fifteen or twenty of the best armed and most to be relied on, in front, who generally approached the houses as fast as their horses could run; this was for two purposes, to prevent their escape and strike terror to the inhabitants—on this account I never got to the houses, after leaving Mrs. Whitehead's until the murders were committed, except in one case. *I some-*

*times got in sight in time to see the work of death com-
pleted, viewed the mangled bodies as they lay, in silent
satisfaction, and immediately started in quest of other victims
. . ."* [Emphasis added].

As for Styron's central thesis that Nat showed irresolution
because he only killed Margaret Whitehead, one can only
say that this is a manifestation of his refusal to understand.
"General Nat," as he is sometimes called, was the *leader* of
the Southampton insurrection, and generals seldom kill. It
was Nat's duty to organize, command, and lead. If Styron
finds this incomprehensible, the explanation is to be sought
not in Nat Turner's inability to kill but in William Styron's
inability to understand a black man leading.

After all, Styron makes Thomas Gray say to Nat, ". . . it
ain't as if you had been *disinvolved* in these proceedings—a
field general runnin' the whole show from way behind the
lines. . . ." In fact, as Gray's *Confessions* makes clear, Nat
was a field general who divided his forces and coordinated
them. "By this time," he says in the Gray *Confessions*, "the
six who had gone by Mr. Bryant's, rejoined us, *and informed
me they had done the work of death assigned them. We
again divided, part going to Mr. Richard Porter's, and from
thence to Nathaniel Francis', the others to Mr. Howell
Harris', and Mr. T. Doyles. On my reaching Mr. Porter's, he
had escaped with his family. I understood there, that the
alarm had already spread, and I immediately returned to
bring up those sent to Mr. Doyles, and Mr. Howell Harris';*
the party I left going on to Mr. Francis', having told them I
would join them in that neighborhood. . . . I immediately
pursued the course taken by the party gone on before; . . .
I pursued on their tracks to Capt. Newit Harris', where I
found the greater part mounted, and ready to start; the men
now amounting to about forty, shouted and hurraed as I
rode up . . ." [Emphasis added].

This is, I submit, the picture of a field commander. And it
was this field commander who initiated the rebellion by

striking his master with a hatchet. Because of the dark, Nat says, "I could not give a death blow, the hatchet glanced from his head" (Styron says Nat "missed by half a foot") and "Will laid him dead." After this incident, Nat directed the rebellion with a light ceremonial sword appropriate to his rank. He struck several blows with this sword but did not kill anyone, he says, "as the sword was dull." Nat's one confirmed kill corroborates this assertion. After repeated blows with the dull sword, he finally picked up a fence rail and dispatched Margaret Whitehead. It is curious that Styron, the white liberal, refuses to accept an explanation which was readily accepted by Thomas Gray, who saw Nat and who described the sword as a light one.

The same thing can be said of Styron's theory that "it was the niggers" that beat Nat. Thomas Gray, who would have seized on evidence of this nature, did not report massive slave resistance to Turner's foray. Nor did contemporary newspaper accounts which said, according to Howison, that Nat was defeated by the real "heroism" of the whites.

Oblivious to this evidence, Styron pursues Nat into his prison cell and deprives him of the meaning of his mission. The caged Nat, according to Styron, was remorseful, contrite, filled with "a terrible emptiness." He couldn't pray; he couldn't talk to God. He was alone and forsaken. Thomas Gray, who visited Nat in prison, contradicts Styron's fantasy. Gray tells us that Nat was calm and cool to the end.

"Do you not find yourself mistaken now?" Gray asked Nat.

"Was not Christ crucified?" Nat answered.

Gray was impressed. "The calm, deliberate composure with which he spoke of his late deeds and intentions, the expression of his fiend-like face when excited by enthusiasm, still bearing the stains of the blood of helpless innocence about him; clothed with rags and covered with chains; yet daring to raise his manacled hands to heaven, with a spirit soaring above the attributes of man; I looked on him and my blood curdled in my veins."

In the 428 pages of William Styron's *Confessions,* there is not one single image to compare with Gray's image of the defiant black rebel raising his manacled hands to heaven.

The difference in tone between the *Confessions* of Gray, the racist, and Styron, the white liberal, gives one pause. Gray, who loathed Nat but who looked into his eyes, gives him to history unrepentant, courageous, sure of his act and his eventual vindication. Styron, who says he sympathizes with Nat, destroys him as a man and as a leader. And the terrifying implication of this fact is that the fascination-horror of a bigot may be more compelling than the fascination-anxiety of a white liberal.

Beyond all that, the two *Confessions* demonstrate how white Americans use black Americans, no matter what we do. When we refrain from cutting throats, they stigmatize us as bootlicking Sambos. And when we cut throats, they make us a Book-of-the-Month-Club selection and give us white dreams and the vocabulary of U. B. Phillips.

It's heads I win and tails you lose. That's the name of William Styron's game. And one comes at the end to the depressing conclusion that Styron's *Confessions* is the worst thing that has happened to Nat Turner since Nat's Last White Man (save one with the pen) broke his neck with a rope on a gallows in a Virginia town called Jerusalem.

The prophet who died in the Jerusalem of America, cool and calm, sure of the Black Resurrection, still awaits a literary interpreter worthy of his sacrifice. He still awaits an interpreter who will not deal himself out of the game, an interpreter who is prepared to give something and to give up something, an interpreter who recognizes that the rope has two ends and that you have to bring a man to find a man.

CHAPTER II

THE CONFESSIONS OF NAT TURNER

AND THE DILEMMA OF
WILLIAM STYRON

ALVIN F. POUSSAINT, M.D.

The Confessions of Nat Turner by William Styron would be more appropriately titled: "The *Imaginations* of William Styron on the Life of Nat Turner." The author himself, in a note at the beginning of his book, states, ". . . in those areas where there is little knowledge in regard to Nat, his early life, and the motivations for the revolt (and such knowledge is lacking most of the time), I have allowed myself the *utmost freedom of imagination* in reconstructing events . . ." [Emphasis added]. No one objects to a novelist using the best of his imagination to write a work of fiction that will have color and saleability. However, Styron is a southern white man who has been raised in a racist society and is not free from the impact of its teachings. How will we ever know how well the author has freed himself of his own white supremacist attitudes as he attempts to project himself into the mind of a black slave?

In the author's note quoted above Styron refers to Nat Turner simply as "Nat." Is this familiarity by the author part of intuitive white condescension and adherence to southern racial etiquette? Is this reference and the entire book an unconscious attempt to keep Nat Turner "in his place"—to emasculate him? Would the novelist expect Nat Turner to address him as "Mr. Styron"? Perhaps no one can ever know the answers to these questions. Yet, they are raised to indicate the potentially profound difficulties that are inherent in Styron's undertaking.

It seems to me that Styron may be guilty of projecting on to Nat Turner many of the classical white stereotypical notions about black people. I am not suggesting that Styron intentionally wished to malign the character and historical significance of Nat Turner. However, through his "imaginations" he unwittingly has selected the types of psychological material which appear to emasculate and degrade Nat Turner and his people. In so doing, the author must accept the responsibility for whatever part his book will play in perpetuating the racist myths of our white society. Since this book has been dubbed an "historical novel" many of the readers will accept the author's "freedom of imagination" as "fact." Thus, the psychological impact on the American public of this widely publicized literary work will be considerable.

For me, *The Confessions of Nat Turner* seems to reveal some obvious and some subtle manifestations of white racist attitudes.

First, almost all of the important and influential persons in our protaganist's early developmental years were white. Even Nat Turner's mother is given a secondary and insignificant role. Instead, those who are portrayed as being most crucial are "Miss Nell, Miss Emmeline, and Marse Samuel." All the people he seemed to "worship" were white. Were there no influential or worthy black people in his life? From the standpoint of current psychological theory one would expect that whatever greatness and strength of character Nat Turner possessed would stem primarily from his early rearing with his mother and father (who are scarcely considered in the book). Yet, the wanderings of Styron's mind seem to focus mainly on his relations with white people. Is this because of a commonly held racist view that a Negro who achieves must be primarily doing so because of his associations with whites? This somewhat disguised theme of "white is right" can be seen in other basic aspects of *The Confessions*.

For example, Nat Turner as a character seems to be quite white. His speech sounds more like Styron's than that of an heroic black slave of nineteenth-century America. In fact, in many places the writer's "imagination" seems to run wild. For example, here is Styron's Nat Turner as he waits on a deserted plantation, "Now, looking down at the shops and barns and cabins and distant fields, I was no longer the grinning black boy in velvet pantaloons; for a fleeting moment instead I owned all, and so exercised the privilege of ownership by unlacing my fly and pissing loudly on the same worn stone where dainty tiptoeing feet had gained the veranda steps a short three years before. What a strange, demented ecstasy! How white I was! What wicked joy!" [page 232]. Is this really our black protagonist speaking, or are we witnessing some sort of vicarious and prurient joy which Styron experiences by projecting this type of imagery into the mind of Nat Turner?

Our hero is also portrayed as a "house nigger" possessing the full range of currently popular and usually overgeneralized feelings of self-hatred, anti-Negro attitudes and a desire to be white which psychiatrists tell us plague black people in a racist culture. However, Nat Turner was a unique and great individual. It could be that what really distinguished him was the fact that he was not indoctrinated with the psyche of a "house nigger." It is just as reasonable, from a psychological viewpoint, to speculate that he did not hate his blackness and that it was self-love that made him a revolutionist revolting against the abominable institution of slavery. There is certainly little in the original confessions of Nat Turner which suggest that he ever played the psychological role of a "house nigger" or "Uncle Tom."[1] Styron's reconstruction of events is an example of the stereotyped belief that black people rebel primarily because of an unful-

[1] See pp. 91–116 of this volume.

filled psychological need to be white and not because of a sense of their own inner dignity. This notion, of course, is the self-flattery of the oppressor who cannot imagine that a black man could want to be anything unless it is an emulation of himself.

And, it follows naturally that if the black man cannot be like the white man then he must certainly yearn for the white woman with an erotic-religious fervor which implies that salvation itself must lie in her loins. This idea is another major psychological theme of *The Confessions.* Once again, Styron presents a Caucasian stereotype of the black man's innermost desires, which is to sexually possess a white woman. This is what the white racists have been telling the black man for centuries. It was the theme of the great racist classic, *The Birth of a Nation,* which glorified the Ku Klux Klan. Therefore, it is not surprising that Styron might sense its appeal to a primarily white American audience.

Why does the author choose to depict Nat Turner as a celibate pining for white women? There is at least one historical account which indicates that he was married to a black slave girl.[2] In the original *Confessions* there is nothing to suggest that our protagonist or his followers were desirous of sexually possessing white female flesh! In fact, Turner and his troops did not sexually molest or rape any white woman whom they had slain or encountered. As anyone acquainted with the behavior of conquering soldiers will testify, this is amazing self-restraint for a band of "drunken" and "undisciplined" black troops. Why didn't these white-women-hungry slaves take advantage of their opportunity? Why does Styron in his tale go so far in distorting the actual historical facts?

The author takes the one recorded fact, that the only person Nat Turner actually killed himself was Miss Margaret Whitehead, and uses this to spin an enormous tale of Turner's

[2] Howard Meyer, *Colonel of the Black Regiment: The Life of Thomas Wentworth Higginson,* New York, 1967, p. 156.

overwhelming, erotic, and quasi-religious attachment to this young girl and her "whiteness." In the novel, even as Nat Turner is going to his death he is still languishing for her white body. In fact, the writer makes it appear as if our black rebel's strength and wish to revolt somehow stemmed mainly from his associations (both real and fantasied) with Miss Margaret. On the last page of the novel as Turner is being led to his execution he is quoted as saying, ". . . I would have done it all again. I would have destroyed them all. Yet I would have spared one. I would have spared *her that showed me Him* whose presence I had not fathomed or maybe never even known" [Emphasis added]. It is clear that from this passage and from others throughout the novel, Styron feels that Nat Turner's emotional attachment to this white "forbidden fruit" was a key factor in his psychological motivation.

Once again we see propagated the hackneyed racist belief that Negroes who are strong, successful, and masculine must also want to possess a white woman in order to give final sanction to their manhood. Why is not the author able to "imagine" that Nat Turner had a young, feminine, beautiful, and courageous black woman who stood by his side throughout his heroic plan to revolt against slavery!?

I think Styron's selection of "factual" and psychological material speaks for itself. It speaks for itself again when we read that the closest our black rebel comes to a realized sexual experience is through a homosexual one with another young black slave. What is the communication here? Naturally, it implies that Nat Turner was not a man at all. It suggests that he was unconsciously really feminine. Styron underscores this image by depicting Turner as a bungling, awkward soldier who is unable to kill his oppressors and pukes at the sight of blood during combat. Thus, throughout the book he is revealed as an emasculated and "abnormal" character. There is even the suggestion here that the rebellion was participated in reluctantly by the "sensitive" Nat

Turner who really only wished to sleep with Miss Margaret to salvage his manhood. The depiction of the young rebel as a would-be deviant carries the implication that the whole revolt against slavery and racism was somehow illegitimate and "abnormal." The author on some level must realize the implications of presenting this type of psychological material to his readers.

I am puzzled as to why Styron in his "imaginations" found it necessary to degrade and emasculate the character of Nat Turner. I have no reason to believe that this was his conscious intention, for in many parts of the novel I detect a strong empathy which the author has for his protagonist. In his foreword to the book he writes, ". . . it has been my own intention to try to re-create a man and his era, . . ." Yet, given the facts and content of the novel, one wonders if Styron was an unwitting victim of his own unconscious white racism for which he alone can not be held fully accountable.

CHAPTER III

YOU'VE TAKEN MY NAT AND GONE

VINCENT HARDING

IN THE COURSE of a *Newsweek* interview celebrating the publication of his latest novel, William Styron said, "I want the book to exist on its own terms as an American tragedy. . . . And I certainly don't mean to indiscriminately glorify the figure of the Negro rebel against society today." Then he added, "You can see Nat Turner as an archetypal American tragic hero, but this doesn't make Rap Brown an archetypal American hero, nor does it make what he is preaching capable of anything but disaster."

As one ponders these and other words attributed to Styron, as we explore the glossy surfaces and the ambiguous substructure of *The Confessions*, it becomes painfully clear that this semi-fictional work and its author's gratuitous comments are indeed part of our long rehearsal in tragedy. But it is also evident that Styron—true to one element of the tragic figure—speaks and writes without comprehension of either the meaning of the drama, or the profound and bitter depths through which America continually moves towards the creation of a thousand Nat Turners more real than his could ever be. For he is obviously convinced that he has discriminately "glorified" the Nat Turner of history, that he has built this strange black mystic into a true hero, and that he has thereby attained the right to judge other dark rebels and their role in America today.

This set of dangerous misapprenhensions is only the beginning of our sorrows, for they are compounded by the host of critics who have joyously proclaimed that Styron has finally done the impossible—entered starkly white into a black man's skin and mind—and has in the course of his impossible feat created a major work of American fiction. (That these critics have been—with one significant exception—also white is, of course, part of our unspeakable dilemma. That *they* should be called upon by journals and reviews to decide when successful penetration of blackness has been accomplished is another parable of our pain.)

How shall one speak of such things in any sense other than the tragic, especially if we attribute some scintilla of well-meaning beneficence to William Styron and his non-critics? For as I sat, black and increasingly anguished, experiencing Styron's audacious attempt to recreate his own Nat Turner out of the sparse materials of history and out of the strangeness of his creative dreams, I could not escape one terrible, constant impression—the overwhelming presence of failure. Or was it something worse than failure? Perhaps so, for the subtitles which came most regularly to my mind were "The Annihilation of Nat Turner" and "The Emasculation of Prophet Nat" (that last being intended in its most obvious sense and more).

No other conclusion seems sensible if one takes the basic historical document (Turner's own dictated *Confessions*) with the seriousness claimed by Styron. There, although the context is limited, Turner leaps forth as a religious mystic, a single-minded black believer with a powerful sense of messianic vocation. He fits well into the apocalypticism of much antebellum religious thought in America, and he is an impressive leader of men. Almost against his own will, Thomas Gray, the white Virginia lawyer who took down the original *Confessions* ends the transcription of Nat's words with his own remarkable testimony. He says he sees in Turner, "The calm, deliberate composure with which he spoke of his late deeds and intentions, the expression of his fiend-like face when excited by enthusiasm, still bearing the stains of the blood of helpless innocence about him; clothed with rags and covered with chains: yet daring to raise his manacled hands to heaven, with a spirit soaring above the attributes of man; . . ." In response, Gray wrote, "I looked on him and my blood curdled in my veins."

The man reported by Gray far overshadows the character created by Styron. Indeed, it appears that the twentieth-century white Virginian was no less overwhelmed by black Nat Turner than was his nineteenth-century counterpart, but he was evidently not so honest. Instead of admitting to the curdling of blood and letting things stand, William Styron's novel becomes an exercise in domestication, assimilation, and finally destruction. At every crucial point it is almost embarrassingly obvious that Styron is unable to comprehend Nat Turner's real stature and meaning, that he does not perceive Turner's role as a tragic-triumphant hero in the biblical genre.

It is Styron's very attempt to enter the biblical world of the rebel slave which most fully provides a symbol for his total betrayal of the historical Turner. Near the beginning of the work, Styron-Turner says, "Of all the prophets it was Ezekiel with his divine fury to whom I felt closest by kinship . . ." Any careful reading of Turner's own *Confessions* indicates that there is certainly ground for such a conclusion, for Turner surely lived in the world of those divinely obsessed spokesmen, including one Jesus of Nazareth. But Styron's particular choice of Ezekiel is of great significance as an illustration, for it was this prophet above all others in the Old Testament who was driven to enter personally and without reserve into the very words and judgements he spoke. It was Ezekiel who was forced to eat the scroll with the Lord's words, to fill his stomach with the terrible oracles of God until they became "sweet as honey." It was he who had to give up his own wife to death as a sign to the people of Israel.

Now this is precisely what William Styron fails to do with the world and words of Nat Turner. He has been unable to eat and digest the blackness, the fierce religious conviction, the power of the man. He has been kept apart from these realities while attempting to tell the inner tale. As a result of such peculiar self-deception, as a result of his separation from Nat's power and drivenness, William Styron has distorted and broken each major truth of Old Prophet Nat. And he has done it to the strange accompaniment of critical applause for his "total integration" into Turner's world. Thus the whitened appropriation of our history by those who have neither eaten nor mourned goes on, tragic because it is not recognized for what it is: a total negation of our power and our truth, indeed an ultimate betrayal of all creative power and liberating truth.

We see the difficulty emerging early in Styron's handling of Nat Turner's secular and religious education in childhood. While Turner, in his *Confessions* to Gray, attributes almost all of his early religious inspiration and teaching to his parents and, especially, his grandmother, Styron totally eliminates this source in his novel. In the fictional work Turner's grandmother dies before the boy's birth, and his mother and father are relegated to negligible roles in the matter of instruction. A white family—particularly the young women in that family—replace them as Turner's major teachers. Why such a change—one which immediately wrenches Turner out of the unique environment of black religion? Whatever the reason, from that point on Styron-Turner's religious experiences continue to produce a feeling of falseness and lack of power. His life, robbed by Styron of its roots, is somehow neither black nor white, and suffers from the loss of particularity as well as power.

Even more important as a symbol of Styron's degradation

of Nat and his messianic vision is the novelist's handling of one of the major religious rituals—baptism. According to the book, Nat's first experience of self-baptism along with the baptism of another person comes when he is in his late teens, and brings with it his initial sense of calling as a special messenger of God. But the startling development by Styron is that this crucial baptism takes place immediately after Nat has been engaged in homosexual mutual stimulation with a young black friend, Willis, and it is obviously his sense of guilt over the act which drives Nat into the river for baptism. Thus Styron-Turner can say,

> "Lord," I said in a loud voice, "witness these two sinners who have sinned and have been unclean in Thy sight and stand in need to be baptized."
> "Das right Lawd," I heard Willis say.

In his own *Confessions*, Nat Turner referred to only one joint baptism, one involving himself and a white convert named Brantley. Styron has used this event too, but in such a way as to continue the demeaning of Nat Turner. For in the novel Brantley is not only a social outcast among whites, he is a mentally retarded, personally repulsive homosexual whose specialty seems to be the molesting of young boys. Again we see the driving force of his search for baptism not in the power of Nat's religious message or personal charisma, but in Brantley's own sense of futility, fear, and sexually confused guilt. Since there was very little description of Brantley in the historical records, Styron alone chose to create such a pariah-like personality for the one white man who is drawn to Nat Turner's religious teachings. How else can this be read except as an act of diminishing the power of William Styron's black "hero"?

Styron does no better with Turner's blackness than he does with his religious vision, especially in relationship to women. For one of the major destructive continuities in *The Confessions* is Nat's fascination with white women—a fascination entirely of the novelist's own making. Perhaps the insidious nature of Styron's distortion becomes most apparent when one notes that his Nat Turner is able to offer clear and often tender descriptions only of white women, not of blacks. In the realm of sexual desire black women become mere shadows in relationship to the many evocations of silken hair, pale, smooth skin, and white, white lives. In his almost overwhelming erotic fantasies—from adolescence to his death—only one black woman appears to Nat Turner as an object of desire, and she is finally pierced only by his tongue.

On the other hand (and every black admirer of Styron's work must speak to this set of contrivances), two white women are introduced into the novel's structure for no other evident purpose than to become the objects of Nat's fierce sexual longing. Even beyond all of this there exists one of the most significant distortions of the historical Nat Turner: Styron's creation of Nat's strange love affair with a teen-age white girl. What manner of black commander is this, whose major heterosexual activities—even in fantasy—are with white women? Is this a heroic black leader who finally helps to destroy his movement because of his weakness for white flesh? Since this major theme and its supporting scenes are entirely of Styron's creation, the questions belong to him alone. Whose mind has he entered save his own?

Nor do any of the other black men in the novel fare much better, something which might have been expected from an examination of the one-dimensional Negroes in some of Styron's other work. Perhaps most obvious and suggestive is Styron's insistence that Will, the slave who kills more regularly than any other, must be a demented, lecherous wild man. Is it only sex and insanity which can motivate a black man to such a large-scale assault on white lives? Is this an attempt to deny the present as well as the past?

But it is the loss of religious center with which I am most concerned, for religion was evidently the focus of Turner's own life. There is in Styron's work no black messiah, no true lover of Ezekiel, not even a superior religious exhorter. For though William Styron-Turner talks about religion a great deal and though he quotes biblical passages in excellent style, the "divine fury" of Old Testament experience is almost totally absent. Though Nat Turner is a preacher, only one major attempt at a sermon is made in *The Confessions,* and it fails to catch any of the peculiar rhythmic and thematic strengths of this black folk art form. Equally striking is the fact that the religious music of Afro-Americans never enters as a major structural element of the novel as one would expect if such a work had been done by an Ellison, a Baldwin, or a Wright.

No, black Prophet Nat has failed to make this scene. The Old Testament is present only as a collection of words in *The Confessions.* There is no wrestling with angels, no anguished groping after God. There is nothing in any way equal to the terse power found in Robert Hayden's poem, "Ballad of Nat Turner." The only wrestling we see in Styron-Turner is with the ephemeral bodies of white women, with the very real penis of a black man, and with his own confused and confusing fears. If any of these is sincerely meant to contribute to the glorification or clarification of the portrait of Nat Turner, then we are surely in the realm of tragedy (almost tragi-comedy). For they only contribute to our picture of a wretched precursor of the Moynihan report; and *that* is a Nat Turner who is simply not to be found in the astringent report of Lawyer Gray, or in the living traditions of black America.

Perhaps we must now say with charity that it is likely too much to expect a white, twentieth-century American novelist to be able to conceive of the world of a black, Old Testament-type messiah. (William Faulkner, Flannery O'Connor and Robert Penn Warren might have made more interesting attempts, I suspect.) The power of belief, the power of righteous anger, the dynamism emanating from a sense of divinely ordained vocation, the power of blackness—none of these is a hallmark of the major section of current American fiction. Erotic fantasy in the world of unreal women, aborted black-white assimilation, confused and ambiguous sexual organs—these may be the best we can do. And if there is any power in Styron's book it is the power of unfulfilled desire, the power of substance wasted in the dust, of weakness and fear, the power of insanity and the murder of God. As such, the novel has snatched Nat Turner out of the nineteenth century, out of the community of black religious rebels, and placed him totally into our own age of nothingness and fear. Is there any salvation from this, from the implied blind arrogance which performs the act, from the insensitive arrogance which raises the applause?

It is when we speak of salvation and arrogance that the most profound and final degradation of black Nat Turner is revealed. The issue of his salvation is broached in a negative way at the outset of the novel. In his cell shortly after capture Nat confesses a sense of separation from God and says, "There seemed no way at all to bridge the gulf between myself and God." Soon it becomes clear that we are dealing not simply with a sense of separation, but more. For Styron-Turner says, "The sense of His absence was like a profound and awful silence in my brain. Nor was it His absence alone which caused me this . . . feeling of despair . . . instead it was a sense of repudiation I felt, of denial, as if He had turned His back on me once and for all . . ."

This theme appears repeatedly throughout the novel until it builds to a place of dominating significance at the end. What is it that has caused this God-driven man to have to endure these days of separation and repudiation? Why would his God hide His shining face? Finally, the answer comes clear. Nat's God has turned His back because this black leader of rebellion has not admitted his remorse for someone's death. So He waits on Nat to repent. But the repentance demanded is not for the death of helpless, guilt-less white children, not even for the destruction of more than one hundred innocent blacks who were killed in reprisal for his rebellion. No, Styron-Turner's God does not deal in such trivialities. He does not shut the door of heaven for those things. Instead, at the end of the novel it becomes clear that *this* God will not return until Nat repents for the death of one white girl, the same adolescent who has sexually aroused Styron-Turner and supposedly opened in him deep wells of desire and love. This is the girl who becomes his only victim, his sacrifice; and after he has pierced her body with his sword and bludgeoned her head, he circles her lifeless frame like a faithful black dog (all this in the midst of a rebellion he is leading).

This young woman becomes the object of Nat's final fantasy in jail, and once more he sends out his life-giving fluid into the nothingness of delusion. Nevertheless, Styron (is it maudlin ineptitude or sheer mockery?) can have his antihero say, ". . . with tender stroking motions I pour out my love within her; pulsing flood; she arches against me, cries out, and the twain—black and white—are one." In the midst of this love of emptiness, this integration into a dream, Nat is able to repent, and with his repentance his God immediately returns and calls him home. (So baptism *and* extreme unction are devoured by inverted sexuality.) Little Miss Margaret Whitehead, the pure virgin, yet not virgin, the dead recipient of black seed, has become Nat Turner's mediator-mistress. Her arched white body becomes Styron-Turner's pathway to their white, white God.

If this is not tragedy, nothing is. It begins with Styron's belief that such a caricature is really Nat Turner. It is deepened by America's eager acceptance of this uninspired offering of homosexuality, pseudo-religion, and dreams (so wonderfully safe!) of black-white grapplings in the dust as an authentic view from under the black skin. Nevertheless, as with all tragedy, the deepest level is to be found within us —black us. And it was perhaps symbolized by one of our most important artists, James Baldwin. For it was Baldwin who praised his friend's work highly, Baldwin who saw himself in Styron's Turner, and Baldwin who dared to say, "This is the beginning of our common history."

Surely it is nothing of the kind. In spite of Baldwin's largest, kindest hopes, Styron has done nothing less (and nothing more) than create another chapter in our long and common agony. He has done it because we have allowed it, and we who are black must be men enough to admit that bitter fact. There can be no common history until we have first fleshed out the lineaments of our own, for no one else can speak out of the bittersweet bowels of our blackness. On the way to that achievement a crucial direction must surely be found in the words of our so recently departed brother, Langston Hughes. For he spoke to our present condition when he wrote:

> You've taken my blues and gone— . . .
> And you fixed 'em
> So they don't sound like me. . . .
> But someday somebody'll
> Stand up and talk about me,
> And write about me—
> Black and beautiful—
> And sing about me,
> And put on plays about me!
> I reckon it'll be
> Me myself!
> Yes, it'll be me.

Only then will we capture Nat Turner from the hands of those who seem to think that entrance into black skin is achieved as easily as Styron-Turner's penetration of invisible white flesh. Only then may it be possible to transform the powerful suggestions of Robert Hayden's marvelous poem about Nat Turner into a full-orbed and faithful encounter with this compelling but mysterious black man. Then we shall judge him for ourselves, and brother Rap will be free to draw his own conclusions—if he is still interested. Then even the Styrons may sense some solid intimation of our darkly glowing, tragic depths. At that moment, as possessors of our own past, we shall have claimed the right to go on with fear and the trembling of joy into whatever divine fury lies ahead on these white and maddening shores. Only then shall common history—and common destiny—begin.

CHAPTER IV

THE CONFESSIONS OF
WILLIE STYRON

JOHN OLIVER KILLENS

AFTER FAITHFULLY PLODDING THROUGH the Number-One Best Seller, *The Confessions of Nat Turner*, after reading all the ballyhoo and pretentious interviews in *The New York Times Book Review* and in *Newsweek* about the book and its author and its author's attitudes vis-à-vis Nat Turner and the writing of the book and black folk generally, I too have a confession to make. I had this uncomfortable feeling that a hoax was being perpetrated against the American reading public. I also had the uneasy feeling, even worse, that the reading public dearly loved it. Like a whore being brutally ravished and loving every masochistic minute of it.

Americans loved this fake illusion of reality because it legitimatized all of their myths and prejudices about the American black man, and further, because it cut yet another great American black man down to the size of a boy. Nat Turner, in the tradition of most black Americans, was a man of tragedy, a giant, but William Styron has depicted him as a child of pathos.

We black Americans are essentially a people of tragedy. Tragedy and irony and paradox have been the core of our existence, slaves and pariahs, in this homeland of the brave and free. The founding fathers, including Washington and Jefferson, held our foreparents in bondage. Thus those greatest of "revolutionaries" were, in grim reality, freedom-loving slavemasters. Thus began all those millions of *little white lies* manufactured through the years to rationalize the Western Paradox and the Great American Tragedy. But perhaps it is impossible for white Americans to see black men in a tragic light; to grant to the black man epic and heroic proportions; to admit to the reality of Afro-American manhood.

Even a consummate tragedian like Sir Lawrence Olivier saw Othello in pathetic terms in the recent movie version of *Othello.* Here was Shakespeare's magnificent Moor reduced to a shuffling stupid-cunning whining idiot, half man and half faggot, which was hardly the kind of characterization that the great bard had in mind (or was it?). Nevertheless, the men of Hollywood were so impressed with the sham Othello, they almost gave Sir Lawrence an Academy Award. On Broadway, in the forties, Paul Robeson gave Othello tragic and heroic proportions. He shook the stage with his powerful performance. But Sir Lawrence made him into a whimpering, pathetic figure. Notwithstanding, Shakespeare *did in fact* write a tragedy, and tragedies do not wallow in pathos. Perhaps Olivier, like most white people, sees the black man as essentially pathetic, but Robeson saw the basic and profound tragedy of black life. God knows he's certainly lived his tragedy. Out of the fundamental truths of our lives we black folk live with tragedy every moment of our existence. Irony and paradox and tragedy. Most men came to America to be free. We came in chains, were brought here to be slaves. There is the irony. And there is the basic cause for Nat's rebellion. There is the fundamental cause of the current black rebellions in the northern cities, the so-called Long Hot Summers. Dreiser wrote *An American Tragedy,* an excellent novel, but the great American tragedies will be written by black Americans. The great American tragedy is black tragedy. Repeat: We black folk live with tragedy. We inhale tragedy with our every breath.

William Styron, darling of the liberal critics, inheritor of the mantle bequeathed to him by 'Sippian Willie Faulkner,

like his namesake, Marse Willie, has not been able to transcend his southern-peckerwood background. The title of this
novel should have been *The Confessions of Willie Styron,*
because that is precisely what the novel is all about. It re-
veals more about the psyche of the "southern liberal" Styron,
direct descendant of ol' Massa, than it even begins to reveal
about the heart and soul and mind of black revolutionary
Nat Turner.

He has attempted to write this novel about the great Nat
Turner out of the consciousness of a slave master, albeit
a "kindly slavemaster," which from the point of view of
the slave was a contradiction in terms. To the revolutionary
slave, there were no "good masters" save those who had
gotten the cold cold ground that was coming to them. Just as
it was impossible for the slave master to look at slavery from
the point of view of the slave, it has proven impossible for
the slave master's grandson to look at slavery or at the contemporary black-and-white confrontation from the perspec-
tive of Rap Brown and Stokely Carmichael or Floyd
McKissick or any other black revolutionary, or black non-
revolutionary, for that matter. The first mistake was for Styron to attempt the novel. It seems to me that the second
mistake William Styron made was to pretend to tell the story
from the point of view of Turner, and it was a colossal error,
one that required tremendous arrogance. And naiveté. Any-
body who believes in "good masters" and "benevolent slavery," or any other euphemisms manufactured to justify
American slavery, is in deep literary trouble when he tries
to motivate the leader of a slave revolt.

Styron has Nat Turner rating slave masters somewhat like
the weekly ratings of television shows—"from the saintly
(Samuel Turner) to the all right (Moore) to the barely toler-
able (Reverend Eppes) to a few who were unconditionally
monstrous." These are not the thoughts of a revolutionary
slave. To him, a master was a master was a master. And any
man who owned another man, who had the say of life and

death of another human being, was not considered saintly.
Styron's preconceptions of black inferiority prevent him
from seeing the black man as total man, prevent him from
seeing American slavery as the cruelest, most inhuman,
slavery system in the entire recorded history of man's bestiality to man. To Styron, the blacks were an inferior race, as
a group, but Nat was different, something special. But I've
heard that song so many times, and in *these* times. "You're
not like the others. You're all right. You're different. You're
almost as superior as the white man."

Here are two irreconcilable moralities: the slavemaster's,
to maintain slavery (blatant or benevolent) at any cost; the
slave's, to utterly destroy the slavery system by every and
any means. The master's ethics are always *enslavement;* the
slave's are ever *liberation*. The liberator is the moral man.

What's the big mystery about Nat's motivation? He was a
slave, PERIOD, which meant, no matter how you sugar-coated
it, he was a non-man. Every slave is a potential revolutionary. The only reason Styron failed to see this fundamental
truth is that the color of Nat's skin stood in the way. The
most obvious way for a non-man to become a man is to wreak
violence upon the men who have raped him of his manhood.
Let me speak plainly. Every black American, then and now,
was and is, a potential Nat Turner. As Margaret Walker
writes in her powerful novel about slavery, *Jubilee:* "No
matter what a white planter said, every slave craved his freedom." This is the fundamental truth that most white men
refuse to face. And the failure to face this truth is the fundamental failure of Styron's *Confessions*.

If Styron really wanted to understand what went into the
making of a Nat Turner, he might have gotten some valuable
hints from Arna Bontemps' tremendous and perceptive
novel, *Black Thunder,* story of a slave conspiracy led by one
Gabriel Prosser in the summer of 1800, the very year Nat
Turner was born, and in his home state of Virginia. Writing
his novel in 1936, Mr. Bontemps finds no terrible problems

with the question of motivation. Here is a brief scene from
Black Thunder:

> Gabriel stood above the thin waisted brown girl, his foot
> on the edge of the bench, one elbow on his knee.
> "It's a man's doings, Juba. You ain't obliged to keep fol-
> lowing along."
> "I hears what you say."
> "The time ain't long, and it's apt to get worse and
> worser."
> "H'm."
> "And it's going to be fighting and killing till you can't
> rest, befo' it's done."
> "I know," she said.
> "And you still wants to follow on?"
> "Yes."
> "Well, it ain't for me to tell you no, gal."
> "I'm in it. Long's you in it, I'm in it too."
> "And it's win all or lose all—on'erstand?"
> "I'm in too. Win all or lose all."
> Mingo stood by listening. He listened to Gabriel's words
> and Juba's short answers and tried to tear himself away.
> Somehow he couldn't move. It was win all or lose all. He
> became pale with that peculiar lavender paleness that
> comes to terrified black men. There was death in the off-
> ing, death or freedom, but until now Mingo had thought
> only in terms of the latter. . . .
> He looked at Gabriel's face, noted the powerful resolu-
> tion in his expression. He looked at Juba and saw that she
> was bewitched. She would indeed follow to the end. He
> was a free Negro and these were slaves, but somehow he
> envied them. Suddenly a strange exaltation came to his
> mind.
> "Yes," he said, breaking into their conversation. "It's
> win all or lose all. It's a game, but it's worth trying and I
> got a good notion we can win. I'm free now, but it ain't
> no good being free when all yo' people's slaves, yo' wife
> and chilluns and all."
> "A wild bird what's in a cage will die anyhow, sooner

or later," Gabriel said. "He'll pine himself to death. He just is well break his neck trying to get out."

This is the dialogue of desperate men, who are ready to go for broke, men who are ready to write a tragedy with their lives, men desperate enough to make a revolution. No pathos here, but ethos abounds. They knew the odds were against them. But over a thousand of them gathered that night and they might have made it, for a time at least, they might have made Nat's rebellion look like an exercise in tiddlywinks, had not the weather interfered and had not one of the slaves panicked and informed his master. There was a storm that night that reached hurricane proportions and flooded creeks and washed away bridges. Black men were brought to trial and hanged. In Bontemps' *Black Thunder*, General John, one of Gabriel's co-conspirators, watched Gabriel as he faced the scaffold silently, even proudly. General John was next. General John thinks to himself: "Was I a singing man, I'd sing me a song now, he thought. I'd sing me a song about lonesome, about a song-singing man long gone. No need crying about a nigger what's about to die free. I'd sing me a song me."

Available documents of that period tell us how the white Virginians grudgingly marveled at the manifest sense of right and contempt for danger shown by Gabriel and his black brothers-in-conspiracy. Reputedly, when Gabriel was asked what he had to say to the court in his defense, he replied: "I have nothing more to offer than what General Washington would have had to offer, had he been taken by the British officers and put to trial by them. I have ventured my life in endeavouring to obtain the liberty of my countrymen, and am a willing sacrifice to their cause; and I beg, as a favour, that I may be immediately led to execution. I know that you have predetermined to shed my blood, why then all this mockery of a trial?"

Styron very slyly entitled his novel, *The Confessions of*

Nat Turner, evoking the image that his novel was a kind of novelized accounting of Nat's own signed and sealed confession. *This has got to be the way it was because Nat, himself, said so.* First of all, we know what confessions of black men are worth in *these times* in the dear old southland. We know how these confessions are brought about and with what methods of persuasion. And we can just imagine what the methods for getting confessions must have been like way back there in the good old days of slavery. So that we would not rely too heavily on Nat's so-called confession as having been wrung from him of his own free will. But even if we take his "confessions" seriously, there is nothing in his "confessions" which suggests some of the "poetic" liberties William Styron takes with the life of this great revolutionary.

For example, there is nothing that suggests that Nat had no love whatever for black women, which is how Styron depicts him. As a matter of fact, he was married to one, but you wouldn't know it from the novel. There is nothing in the record to suggest Nat's great lust and passion for white women, but this is the way he is presented throughout Styron's novel. Even in the end, just before he goes to the gallows, he is not thinking about his people's freedom or his own death. He is having this fantasy with this pure white-as-the-driven-snow Missy Margaret Anne.

> . . . And now . . . beyond my dread and emptiness, I feel the warmth flow into my loins and my legs tingle with desire. I tremble and I search for her face in my mind, seek her young body, yearning for her suddenly . . . with a craving beyond pain; with tender stroking motions I pour out my love within her; pulsing flood; she arches against me, cries out, and the twain—black and white—are one. I faint slowly. . . .

So now you know what Nat's Rebellion was all about. Nat had a thing for white women. And of course, the analogy for

our times is that this is also what the black militants are all
about, the so-called "race rioters," the demonstrations; they
all spring out of one great overwhelming obsession, i.e. to
jump into the bed with Mister Charlie's darling daughter.
Like the southern gentleman of old, Styron is hung up with
the question: "How would you like for one of them to
marry your daughter?" As if marrying Charlie's daughter
is how the American Negro became the most multicolored
race on earth. As if Uncle Tom raping Little Eva was how
"yaller yunguns" came to be.

I searched this book in vain for some evidence that literate Nat Turner had heard of insurrectionist Gabriel Prosser
and revolutionary Toussaint L'Ouverture and Denmark
Vesey. Surely, I thought, Nat had read and been inspired,
yes, inflamed by David Walker's *Appeal . . . to the Colored
Citizens of the World But in Particular and very Expressly
to those of the United States of America*. Walker's *Appeal*
was the most inflammatory indictment of slavery ever written. But there is no hint in Styron's *Confessions* that this
pamphlet ever reached the hands of militant Nat Turner.
Possibly it didn't, but most probably it did. Walker's message was not written for free men but for the slaves themselves and by September, 1829, he had devised means to get
it into their hands. He called on them to revolt, to over-
throw slavery by any means necessary. He even frightened
some of the dedicated white abolitionists, who thought that
he had gone too far. The question here is: why did not Styron use Walker's *Appeal* as a part of Turner's motivation?
Was he unaware of it? Or was he trying to give the impression that there was little evidence of unrest amongst the
black folk? And that Nat Turner was some kind of freak
among his brethren?

Styron's *Confessions* has Nat thinking, as he tries to instill
black militancy into his fellow co-conspirators: "Lord, how I
strove to drive the idea of a nigger Napoleon into their

ignorant minds!" And I would ask, why did not Nat think to inspire them with an example of black militancy in the person of black Toussaint, who liberated a nation of black folk from the colonial rule of the same Napoleon?

Styron maintains that Nat's was the only effective slave revolt in the annals of American slavery. Here again the implications are that the slaves were on the whole a docile lot, thereby evoking the hackneyed image of kindly masters and of happy and contented black folk wallowing in their degradation like pigs in a pool of mud and sunlight. But the records are full of black uprisings, plots and rumors of plots, from New York to South Carolina and Georgia, Virginia, Maryland, Mississippi.

On a Sunday evening in September of 1739, Cato led a band of black avenging angels in Stono, South Carolina, and left a trail of blood (white men's) all along the countryside, killing all within their wake. The point is: Many of the slaves did not feel compelled to act out the role ol' Massa had written in the script for them. Some hadn't even read the script, being, as they were, illiterate. The slaves were so "contented" the slavemasters could not afford the astronomical cost of fire insurance. Dear old Dixieland was in a constant state of insurrection. Thousands of rapturous slaves killed their mistresses and their masters, put spiders in the Big House soup, broke their farming implements accidentally-on-purpose, set fire to the cotton patches, and, all in all, demonstrated their contentedness in most peculiar ways.

I'm saying that the great Nat Turner must be seen in this kind of revolutionary context, to be properly understood, and to properly understand what is happening in the northern urban areas. I'm saying that just as "kindly masters" could not save the day during the good old genteel days of slavery, Great White Fathers will not be able to stem the tide of revolution today by joining (even leading) in the singing of "We Shall Overcome." The "natives" are in a restive mood again, and nothing short of total liberation will

quench their thirst for freedom. There are thousands of Nat
Turners in the city streets today, and the ranks of freedom-
fighters are increasing every moment.

I don't say that William Styron is dishonest. I imagine
he is as honest as he can be, granted his racial backwardness.
I'm saying that it is impossible for the slavemaster's grandson to see the revolutionary black man in the sense that
Gabriel saw himself, as the "George Washington" of his
people, ready to lay down his life for their liberation. I repeat: What we have in this new novel, is not the confessions
of Nat Turner, but rather the confessions (unintentional to
be sure) of Master William Styron, White Anglo-Saxon
Southern Protestant. Moreover they are confessions which
reveal that Styron has progressed but a very short distance
from the attitudes of his grandfather. He is still in desperate
need of emancipation from his slavemaster's psychology. He
remains until this very day an unreconstructed southern
rebel.

What about the quality of the writing in Styron's *Confessions?* It is inspired, in spots, dull and repetitious oftentimes,
tiresome even, jumping back and forth in time and space.
And, in terms of getting into the slave's psyche and his
idiom, it is a monumental failure. Then there was this contradiction of Nat, himself, sometimes thinking and speaking
in biblical or Victorian English and at other times lapsing
into an Amos-and-Andy dialect. But Styron misses entirely
the beauty of Afro-American idiom, which has very little to
do with accent, but has everything to do with the rhythms
and mannerisms of black language, the manners of formula-
tions and of thinking through and the special way of saying
things, the unique-to-our-blackness methods of expression;
the Afro-American psyche. Amos-and-Andy dialect is easy,
too easy. On the other hand, black idiom, Afro-Americanese,
is more difficult to achieve, but it is also more authentic,
more rewarding and profound; it is historic and creative.
Styron, in attempting to write Afro-Americanese, is like a

man who tries to sing the blues when he has not paid his dues.

Styron tells us *about* the story of Nat Turner, but he is not *of* the story, and the reader does not feel it, does not live it, for the simple reason that the author has not felt it, has not lived the reality of being black in a white supremacist society. A profounder, more perceptive artist will not only make the reader believe the story happened, but that it is happening at the moment he is reading it. And more, that he is happening along with it. This kind of urgent immediacy is completely missing in Styron's *Confessions.* His style, structure, and perception (or lack of it) utterly defeat immediacy. He explains the situations, and the reader gets the feeling it is not a lived experience.

Styron says Hiram Haydn, then editor at Random House, advised him years ago against attempting *Nat Turner.* "I don't think you have a real understanding of the thing." It was very sound advice. And the years did not equip the author with any deeper understanding. This is all just a way of saying that the story of Nat Turner is still to be written, and it will be up to a black man to write *this* great American tragedy.

Black brothers and sisters, be not deceived by the obscene weeping and gnashing of teeth by white America over the assassination of our great black brother and Messiah, Martin Luther King. They loved him not, or he would still be here amongst us. They understood him not. Our Martin was a revolutionary, and they did not dig him; therefore they destroyed him.

Only the black brethren can really understand the deepest meaning of the "Long Hot Summers," the man sentenced for centuries to non-manhood, here and now affirming manhood for all men and for all times, heroically reaffirming the birthright of everyman, the right of revolution. I am not yet an advocate of Burn, Baby, Burn, but unlike Willie Styron, I dig the motivation of the valiant freedom-fighters.

CHAPTER V

THE MANIPULATION OF HISTORY AND OF FACT: AN EX-SOUTHERNER'S APOLOGIST TRACT FOR SLAVERY AND THE LIFE OF NAT TURNER; OR, WILLIAM STYRON'S FAKED CONFESSIONS

JOHN A. WILLIAMS

A GOOD ARTIST is never satisfied; he breaks his own mold and works to create new ones. He tests new styles, new experiences. He is willing to explore the outermost limits of human experience, even those alien to him, suffering his imagination to be his guide. Many critics and readers believe William Styron has done just this as a writer in his latest novel, *The Confessions of Nat Turner*. Why? Because he, a white man and a southerner, employing the first person, put himself in the place of a black man. Not just *a* black man, but a very special one who lived one hundred thirty-six years ago.

Since I do not believe that the right to describe or portray or in other ways delineate the lives of black people in American society is the private domain of Negro writers, I cannot fault Styron's *intent*. White writers by the score have been taking over that function, anyway. Indeed, works by white writers on black people are considered to be more palatable and acceptable to the nation at large than similar works by black writers. I hold John Clellan Holmes' *The Horn* far and away the best work by a white author on Negroes in contemporary times. I wish I had written it. I cannot say that Styron's book was honest; I have doubts that even in intent it was honest.

The premise that Nat Turner's revolt was the "only effective, sustained revolt in the annals of American Negro slavery" forewarns those of us who know something about slave revolts that a whopping big lie or a great blob of ignorance is about to be revealed. What does "sustained" mean? Turner's revolt was but two days in duration. Do we have here the novelist as publicity hack? That is one question. The other is, if not a publicity hack, do we then have here the novelist as a propagandist for a white history that is already dangerously askew?

Historical figures cannot move in a historical vacuum. Is the vacuum surrounding Styron's Nat Turner the result of the failure of the author to thoroughly research his material? A novelist embarked on a historical work becomes a historian in effect, and he must evaluate his character in terms of the time in which his character lived. He is required to be *both* a novelist and a historian, like Robert Graves or Mary Renault or Arna Bontemps. Bontemps' novel, *Black Thunder,* published in 1936, is about the slave leader, Gabriel, who was, coincidentally, hanged for his attempted revolt the very same week Nat Turner was born. Both men were from the same state. The Denmark Vesey revolt in South Carolina occurred when Turner was twenty-two years old. That same year, 1822, slaves were returned to Africa to build a nation now called Liberia. According to Carter G. Woodson in *The Negro in Our History* (6th edition) there were no less than seven *known* revolts during Turner's lifetime, most of them probably to his knowledge. And what happened to the War of 1812 when the British tried to entice slaves away to their lines—just as they had done during

America's rebellion in 1776? These are all points that other contributors to this collection will undoubtedly take up. *My* point is that Styron failed here as a novelist to research the historical influences on his character.

Or did he? It cannot be said that this is the ignorance of all whites when it comes to the Negro past; the majority of books on slave revolts have been written by whites. Could it be that Styron is guilty here of manipulation? The material was available. He did review Herbert Aptheker's book, *American Negro Slave Revolts* in *The New York Review of Books* in September, 1963. If until that time the author had been (1) too lazy or (2) too ignorant to do research, surely Aptheker's book should have warned him that something was amiss; that his underlying theme was based on quicksand. But Styron continued with his premise of Turner and his act's uniqueness. Witness his words on page 387:

> Surely Travis put his trust in the fragile testimony of history, reckoning with other white men that since these people in the long-recorded annals of the land had never risen up, they never *would* rise up, and with this faith—rocklike, unswerving as a banker's faith in dollars—he was able to sleep the sleep of the innocent, all anxieties laid to rest.

Having chosen his theme of "only revolt" (which many critics swallowed quite whole), why then Styron was constrained to edit all other like occurrences to make his theme valid. Whether this was deliberate or the result of being a man of the South does not matter; the end result is exactly the same. Once more the history of black and white, already managed beyond belief, gets another shot of Whitey-Serum.

Heretofore Styron's writings have expressed little but southern regionalism, in the vein of William Faulkner. He is, in fact, Faulkner's successor. But Faulkner would never be found with characters so stock as a Jeremiah Cobb, the hard-drinking, pain-ravaged judge who, we are made to see, understands Turner and what the institution of slavery must inevitably bring to the whites. Yet Cobb can do nothing; he understands, but cannot act. Nor would Faulkner have given us Margaret Whitehead, at once an innocent girl and a little tease. This distant, spider-web-thin affair between Nat and Margaret never really comes into any kind of focus; yet Turner kills her in the novel as he did in real life. The author believes Turner in reality may have been in love with her; this explains the murder. In Faulkner's hands, Turner would have become Lucas Beauchamp, cold, unremitting. But in Styron's hands he becomes, really, a modern black intellectual cast back over one hundred thirty-six years. He is not even an Othello, but a Hamlet fearful that he will lose the ability to act when the time comes. He is also fearful that he will lose command of his troops to Will, a black slave sick with rage at all whites, and, in the losing, fail in the revolt. In real history, not Styron's, Will was almost as patient and self-possessed as Turner. In short, I find the characters to be not the creation of an artist, but the creation of an artist who has never forgotten that he is also a southerner.

In *The Confessions* we also find the apologist theme: free Negroes suffered far more than did slave Negroes. Therefore, the implication goes, slavery wasn't all bad; a slave had food, clothes, and shelter. This theme is repeated a few times in the novel, always in brief, always strongly done. The scene with Isham, the free Negro, and Moore, a white man who owes him a quarter, is most representative. Moore, of course, is a bad man. Who else would remain in twenty-five cents debt to a free Negro whose wife and children are starving? Styron's bad people are bad, and his good people are good and there is very little mix except in Turner.

The language Styron chose to place in Turner's mouth is full-bodied, slow, it seems, and often beautiful. I was not bothered by it—completely. What *did* bother me was that only the Negro characters spoke the real earthy language: "fucker," "cunt," "cuntlapper," "shit," "shiteating." Now, I rather like using four-, six-, eight-, ten-, and twelve-letter curse words; something really gets loose when they are down on paper, something solid about men and words. However Anglo-Saxon these words might be, it does not seem likely that they were employed in the early nineteenth century among the slaves. I don't doubt that there *were* swear words, but not these. Like slang, swear words, certain kinds of them, have a vogue in time. Styron has transplanted the present back into the past.

For all of this there are moments when Styron's Turner casts off Hamlet's image and truly approaches that of Othello before Iago got his hands on the handkerchief, and there were moments when I could almost hear the voice of Paul Robeson speaking the lines. These moments, however, were few. One judges a novel mainly on what it *says*, its theme. This novel, what it *says* is not the way it was or is. If, however, *Black Thunder* were to be published tomorrow, it would not have the slightest chance of making critics and readers reconsider their thoughts on history as it involved slaves. Black writers, it appears, have lost the race, if there ever was one, to air the truth. The likes of Styron are already past the finish line.

CHAPTER VI

THE FAILURE OF
WILLIAM STYRON

ERNEST KAISER

THE PROBLEM of creating Negro characters in historical fiction (within the veil and in slavery) is very difficult even for Negro writers. Margaret Walker's novel *Jubilee* (1967) written after talking with people who knew the early characters and steeping herself in the family history and Arna Bontemps's novel *Black Thunder* (1935, 1964) about Gabriel's Virginia slave insurrection of 1800 are just two examples of this. Du Bois in parts of *The Souls of Black Folk* and James Weldon Johnson's poem "O Black and Unknown Bards" succeed in evoking the slaves' emotional reaction to slavery. Historical fiction about Negroes that has real characters and is true to history is almost impossible even for the most understanding white writers in the racist, separatist United States.

There have been, nevertheless, a few novels dealing with Negro slave uprisings and unrest: Harriet Beecher Stowe's *Dred* (1856), G. P. R. James's *The Old Dominion* (1858), Mary Johnston's *Prisoners of Hope* (1899), Pauline C. Bouve's *The Shadows Before* (1899), A. Bontemps's *Black Thunder* (1935, 1964), Frances Gaither's *The Red Cock Crows* (1944) and Daniel Panger's *Ol' Prophet Nat* (1967). There are also the plays *Nat Turner* by Paul Peters (published in Edwin Seaver's *Cross Section*, 1944) and *Harpers Ferry: A Play about John Brown* (1967) by Barrie Stavis that have been produced in our time. In addition to these works, there were Herbert Aptheker's *American Negro Slave Revolts* (1943) and his 1937 master's thesis at Columbia University (published as *Nat Turner's Slave Rebellion* in 1966) plus a long bibliography in each book. Lately we have had F. Roy Johnson's *The Nat Turner Slave Insurrection* (1966) and John Lofton's *Insurrection in South Carolina: The Turbulent World of Denmark Vesey* (1964). So this was the considerable body of writing available to William Styron when he, in the late 1940's, began to look for material on Nat Turner. Now Finkelstein, in his book *Existentialism and Alienation in American Literature* (1965), calls Styron a disciple of Faulkner and an existentialist whose fiction is technically good but more subjective and narrower in focus than Faulkner's and thus of less significance. Mike Newberry's review of Styron's third novel *Set This House on Fire* (1960) (the other two are *Lie Down in Darkness* [1951] and *The Long March* [1952]) in *Mainstream* (Sept. 1960) calls him a writer of overwhelming ability who is extremely pessimistic and without a moral point of view in this novel. John Howard Lawson, in an essay "Styron: Darkness and Fire in the Modern Novel" (*Mainstream*, Oct. 1960), disagrees somewhat with Newberry. He calls Styron a brilliant and sensitive writer who has moved from the Freudian, psychoanalytic frame of reference of his first novel to the existentialism of the third. Comparing his compassion to Chekhov's in the first novel and his social understanding to that of Thomas Wolfe's last novel *You Can't Go Home Again* in the third, Lawson says that Styron is angry at the evil of the social environment which destroys people but also feels that the trouble is mystical and hidden in the soul. This conflict, he says, creates faults in his writing. Styron, Lawson continues, must face the fact that he is abetting in his writing the corruption of life and art which he passionately opposes and is thus another promising American talent deteriorating like Mailer, James Jones, and others. I would add that *Set This House on Fire* is obviously a very

heavily autobiographical novel like the novels of Thomas
Wolfe. Lawson comments that this third book has anti-Italian,
anti-Semitic, and anti-Negro stereotypes. Cass (Styron), the
central character in the novel, speaks of his nightmares being
tied up with Negroes. His guilt, says Lawson, is specifically
related to his feeling as a white southerner that he has participated in shameful treatment of Negroes.

But when Styron comes to write his fourth novel *The Con-
fessions of Nat Turner* (1967) which has haunted him since
1948, his talent really deteriorates and goes downhill as
Lawson had noted earlier. His social view, instead of de-
veloping, has remained where it was in his third novel or
even gone backward. He has read all of the works on Nat
Turner and slave rebellions and rejected them. Herbert
Aptheker points out in a footnote to his article-review of
Styron's *The Confessions* ("Styron-Turner and Nat Turner:
Myth and Truth," *Political Affairs,* Oct. 1967) that Styron
borrowed a few years ago the manuscript of his master's
thesis written in 1936 and published as *Nat Turner's Slave
Rebellion* in 1966. It was kept several months and then re-
turned. In a review of Aptheker's *American Negro Slave Re-
volts* and Stanley M. Elkins's *Slavery,* Styron attacks
Aptheker's book, retitles and reduces it to *Signs of Slave
Unrest* and the U.S. slaves' organized rebellion to very little.
But he praises highly the Elkins book describing the dehumanized, Sambo slave (*New York Review of Books,* Sept. 28,
1963).

In his article "This Quiet Dust" (*Harper's,* Apr. 1965)
which was reprinted in the book *Best Magazine Articles
1966,* Styron says that he distrusts any easy generalizations
about the South by white sociologists, Negro playwrights,
southern politicians, and northern editors since his own
"knowledge" of Negroes as a southern youth was gained at
a distance through folklore and hearsay. (Why Negro playwrights, who are on the other side of the racial fence, should
be thrown in is beyond me.) Then he proceeds to project his

own generalization that although Ralph Ellison is right about the constant preoccupation of southern whites with Negroes, perpetual sexual tension between Negroes and whites in the South is greatly exaggerated, so effective have been the segregation laws from the 1890's to the present. And this assertion is based solely on his own experiences. But the sociologists, playwrights, and editors (never mind the southern politicians) have better information than mere personal experience on which to base their generalizations. The corollary of Styron's idea of little interracial sex in the South is the mythology that white women are put on pedestals by white men in the South. Harry Golden, a northern liberal now living in the South, believes this along with Styron. He restates the myth in his book *Mr. Kennedy and the Negroes* (1964). Styron admits that there was enormous interracial sex during slavery. (The southerner Ross Lockridge Jr.'s mammoth historical novel *Raintree County* [1948] has the white wife become insane when the white slaver moves his Negro woman into the same house with her.) The article "The Plight of Southern White Women" (*Ebony*, Nov. 1957) says that southern women, told that they were nice ladies by the men, were kept home off juries, away from high-paying jobs and voting booths—out of competition. Also that white women were enslaved along with the Negroes in the South and that the freedom of these two groups has always run closely parallel; that white women were used as a shield behind which white men committed cowardly acts of violence against Negroes; and that southern white women hate playing the roles of Scarlett O'Haras.

Styron's writing of *The Confessions*, he says further in "This Quiet Dust," is an attempt to *know* the Negro. And yet, he rejects here, as he has elsewhere, Aptheker's documented books on American Negro slave revolts when he states baldly that in 250 years of slavery, there were no uprisings, plots or rebellions except those led by Gabriel Prosser in Virginia in 1800, Denmark Vesey in South Carolina in

1822 and Nat Turner in Virginia in 1831. He again accepts wholeheartedly the fraudulent and untenable thesis of Frank Tannenbaum and Stanley M. Elkins (see my refutation in an essay in *Freedomways,* Fall 1967) that American slavery was so oppressive, despotic and emasculating psychologically that revolt was impossible and Negroes could only be Sambos.

The problems of Negro-white relations in the South that come up in Styron's essay reveal the level of his understanding of the Negro problem: he doubts that there are sexual relations to any degree between the races in the segregated South; he explains the question of Nat Turner's intelligence, precocity, and apprehension; he states boldly that Americans believe that the slave system, though morally wrong, was conducted with such charity and restraint that insurrection and murder were unthinkable; he has a constant preoccupation with "knowing" Negroes; and he seems to relish the horrible details of the whites' bestiality toward Negroes. Examples of bestial descriptions in his article are his unnecessary, gruesome explanation that the doctors skinned Nat Turner's dead body, after he was hanged along with 17 other Negroes, and made grease of his flesh; and the lurid details in his novel of the killings of whites by Negroes.

Styron, after having read Aptheker's master's thesis on Nat Turner, puts all the ideas that Aptheker refuted in his essay. Styron says that the greedy cultivation of tobacco caused the economic depression in Tidewater Virginia before 1831; Aptheker says that the fall in the price of cotton caused the disaster. Styron largely accepts W. S. Drewry's book *The Southampton Insurrection* (1900); Aptheker rejects it as untruthful; Styron says that stringent codes for policing slaves followed the revolt; Aptheker says that many of these stringent codes preceded Nat's revolt. Styron says that Virginia was edging close to emancipation; Aptheker's book says that there never was in the South a flourishing emancipation movement. Nat Turner's rebellion in which many whites were killed, says Styron further in this essay, was an act of futility.

It caused about 200 Negroes to be tortured and killed and obviously should never have taken place at all. Aptheker shows that Nat Turner's revolt was the culminating blow of a period of rising slave unrest which began about 1827 and played itself out in 1832; it brought historic social forces to a head. The revolt blew off the lid which the slavocracy had clamped down upon the press and the rostrums of debate and lecture. From then on until the Civil War, continues Aptheker, there was a confrontation of Abolitionists and slavocrats, of North and South. Styron also says that today in southeast Virginia Negroes are living amiably with white paternalism which includes restricting Negroes from owning new-model Buicks or their children from going to school with whites. This is a total lie. I am a native of that part of Virginia and have scores of relatives there who not only carry on large-scale, mechanized farming and own and drive big automobiles if they are able to; they also are activists in the NAACP chapters there, and there have been court suits all over the area in the past several years which have resulted in some desegregation of the public schools in that area. Styron should look at the quarterly *Race Relations Law Reporter* (published at Vanderbilt University School of Law, Nashville, Tenn.) for the last eight years and see the scores of Virginia desegregation cases there.

It is clear from this essay's whole approach to and attitude toward Negroes that Styron has no equipment either factually or psychologically to write a novel about Nat Turner or any other Negro for that matter. His essay is a 20- or 30-year throwback to the racism and paternalism of the 1930's and 1940's. In the author's note in *The Confessions,* Styron says Nat Turner's rebellion was the only effective, sustained revolt in the annals of American Negro slavery. That makes Aptheker's 409-page doctoral dissertation at Columbia University, published as the book *American Negro Slave Revolts* in 1943 and twice since, just a pack of lies! Styron says further in his review of Aptheker's *American Negro Slave*

Revolts mentioned above that the view of the slave as in revolt against slavery is a part of the white man's fantasy. On
the contrary, his view of the slaves as Sambos is but a common variety of southern racist fantasy based on ignorance
and buttressed by Tannenbaum and Elkins's false thesis
while the revolt thesis is based on solid historical research
by Aptheker and many others, Negro and white.

He also says further in his note that his novel is not so
much an historical novel as it is a meditation on history. It
is a meditation all right and that of an unreconstructed
southern racist.

He says in his essay that the novel has a psychoanalytical
emphasis upon Nat's so-called tormented relationship with
his father following psychoanalyst Erik Erikson's book *Young
Man Luther*. Aptheker's article-review of *The Confessions*
shows that while Styron quotes from Turner's *Confessions*,
he also twists certain facts to suit his Freudian thesis in the
novel. In many other cases, says Aptheker, he falsifies the
known facts of Nat Turner's history, and Styron admits in
the author's note that he has allowed himself the utmost
freedom of imagination in reconstructing Turner's early life
and the motivations for the revolt. The unspeakable arrogance of this young southern writer daring to set down his
own personal view of Nat's life as from inside Nat Turner
in slavery! Instead of trying to get the true feeling of the
Negroes of the period as Howard Fast did in *Freedom Road*
(to say nothing of Margaret Walker's and Arna Bontemps's
hard historical work in *Jubilee* and *Black Thunder* respec-
tively), Styron, who doesn't really know the Negroes living
in Virginia today, deigns to speak personally for the slaves.

As Lawson has pointed out, Styron's early novels had only
anti-Negro stereotypes. But *The Confessions* is infinitely
worse. All of the Negro stereotypes are here: the filthy, racist
language of American whites: nigger, nigger, nigger on almost every page, black toadeater, darky, pickininny, ginger-
colored Negro with thick lips. He puts in over and over the

Negro's black color: the white woman's fingers upon the Negro's black arm. Aptheker's article-review also gives many other examples of Styron's despicable, racist descriptions of Negroes. The language of *The Confessions* equals in its vile racist filth that found in J. C. Furnas's *Goodbye to Uncle Tom* (1956) which I pilloried in *Freedomways*, Spring 1961. Other stereotypes in the novel are the servile, cringing slave, the slave who loves his slave-master, the slave craving a white woman and the main stereotype which the whole book points up: the slave who confesses the details of the plot or revolt against slavery for freedom to a white man when caught like a child who has done something wrong against his parents. The ignorant Styron even has the temerity to attempt to explain how much hatred Negroes have for the white man and why. His ignorance and arrogance know no bounds. Like every white southerner, Styron has to know the Negro, as he says in "This Quiet Dust," although he really knows nothing and wants to find out nothing of Negro life and history.

This novel is a witches' brew of Freudian psychology, Elkins's "Sambo" thesis on slavery and Styron's vile racist imagination that makes especially Will and Nat Turner animals or monsters. Styron has to rationalize the oppression of Negroes in one way or another. Elkins says that the American slave system was so oppressive that Negroes had to be Sambos and Freud says that there were dark, ineradicable, primitive drives or instincts in Turner that made him a beast. Aptheker says in his article-review that the fictional image of the Dunning school of history was *The Clansman*, *Gone with the Wind* of the U. B. Phillips school, and William Styron's *The Confessions of Nat Turner* of the Elkins school. Having rejected the Negro people's history, Styron cannot see Turner as the hero he was and as the Negro people see him; as a slave who led a heroic rebellion against the dehumanization of chattel slavery. This novel makes Styron look like a Rip Van Winkle who has slept through the Negro people's twelve-year freedom struggle of the 1950's and 1960's.

But just as Michael Harrington, Jason Epstein, Norman Podhoretz and other reviewers seized upon Elkins's *Slavery* as a rationale of the Negro slave as a "Sambo" personality thus relieving themselves of the great guilt of American Negro chattel slavery; so, as Aptheker has pointed out in his article-review, reviewers of Styron's *The Confessions* have seized upon this book as pointing up the current Negro ghetto uprising as led by mad Negroes, as futile, stupid rebellions which should be put down ruthlessly. Critics Elizabeth Hardwick and Norman Podhoretz have written about the decline of book reviewing in the U.S. into advertising blurbs. Historian Christopher Lasch, in *The New Radicalism in America* (1965), says that journalism has degenerated into public relations, advertising and propaganda. An outstanding literary critic, Stanley Edgar Hyman, in *Standards: A Chronicle of Books for Our Time* (1966), talks about truth as unfashionable in literary journalism. Harry Golden, in an essay in the "What I Have Learned" series (*Saturday Review*, June 17, 1967) states that "journalists are writers who have no education and disdain looking up words in dictionaries or subjects in encyclopedias, relying on their memories." Certainly the decline of book reviewing and the ignorance of journalists are sharply pointed up by the near unanimity of high brow, middle brow, low brow, liberal and conservative reviewers in praising Styron's novel. But they all, with no research behind the novel or historical knowledge of the South in the 1820's and 1830's, seem to be basically approving of the novel's thesis rather than really reviewing the historical novel which they were not equipped to do. As Thomas Lask says in a review of Kenneth Tynan's *Tynan Right and Left* (*New York Times*, Dec. 12, 1967), under the cover of esthetics these reviewers are condemning what they hate in politics or approving what they like.

Newsweek (Oct. 16, 1967) in a cover story called *The*

Confessions an act of revelation to a whole society. Wilfred Sheed, the book review editor of *Commonweal*, in a front page review in *The New York Times Book Review* (Oct. 8, 1967), called the novel artificial but knowing no history he could only accept Styron's view of history; Eliot Fremont-Smith, in a two-part review in the *New York Times* (Oct. 3–4, 1967), also knowing nothing of Negro history, goes all out. He calls the book a triumph, a rare book that shows us our American past, our present, ourselves, compelling, convincing, a rich and powerful novel. The *New Republic's* reviewer was C. Vann Woodward, a historian who has already swallowed Elkins's thesis whole and uncritically in "The Anti-Slavery Myth" (*American Scholar*, Spring 1962). In the Oct. 7, 1967, issue, Woodward repeats the lie that Nat's rebellion was the only slave rebellion of consequence in the largest slave society in the nineteenth century world as well as the Elkins thesis that Negro slaves were servile Sambos. Accepting and repeating all of Styron's slave stereotypes, he says that the novel shows a respect for history and has a sure feeling for Nat's period. Woodward calls the novel the most profound fictional treatment of slavery in our literature embracing all the subtleties and ambivalences of race in the South.

In *The Nation* (Oct. 16, 1967), the reviewer Shaun O'Connell, a young English teacher at the University of Massachusetts, is completely overwhelmed by Styron's novel. Obviously knowing nothing of Negro history, O'Connell accepts all of Styron's false psychological twistings and all of his invented "facts" about Turner's life as valid and sensible. He thinks that Styron, a twentieth century southerner, has really gotten inside a nineteenth century Negro slave and portrayed him accurately. He says that Styron has improved his craft and modulated his style; that *The Confessions* is the best of his novels. He also calls Styron's "This Quiet Dust" an important essay. And all of this is called fiction criticism by *The Nation* editor's note. *The Nation* does carry in

the same Oct. 16th issue "A Note on the History" by Herbert
Aptheker which says more briefly what Aptheker spells out
in his *Political Affairs* (Oct. 1967) article-review on the novel.
And that is plenty as we have seen above. We will only say
here that Aptheker again nails the lie repeated by the historian Woodward and Styron that the Nat Turner revolt was
the only sustained U.S. Negro slave revolt, armed attack or
uprising. He says that there were slave uprisings from 1691
in Virginia to 1864 in Mississippi. He also points out that
Styron lyingly makes a monster of Will who in reality was
not like that at all.

Other reviewers, with no knowledge, just accepted the
novel as accurate. *The National Observer* (Oct. 9, 1967)
headed the review "Fiction Vivifies the Facts of a Tidewater
Tale." Poppy Cannon White, in a review of the book in her
column in the Negro newspaper *New York Amsterdam News*
(Nov. 25, 1967) says that *The Confessions* seems persuasive,
historically accurate, and is a remarkable document. She
says that the hero of the novel looks, sounds, and feels like
truth, but she finds Turner portrayed as a madman hard to
take. The book wallows in violence, she says, but she thinks
of the violence as she thinks of Truman Capote's nonfiction,
violent novel about multiple murder *In Cold Blood* (1965):
these are books, she says, about tortured minds and dark
recesses of the spirit. Mrs. White disagrees about Nat Turner's revolt being the only one; she says that there were
hundreds of revolts. In a later column (Dec. 9, 1967) devoted
to *The Confessions*, she says that she received a lot of mail
about her previous column reviewing the novel; that some
letters agreed and some disagreed with her statement that
Nat's revolt wasn't the only sustained revolt in American
slavery. Mrs. White then contrasts *The Confessions* and
other slave novels with another new novel, Harold Cour-
lander's *The African*, a book, she says, concerned with a man,
with real people who have a past and a culture. *Time* magazine called the book a new peak in the literature of the
South. *Harper's* called it a masterpiece of storytelling. The

historian Arthur Schlesinger, Jr., called the book in *Vogue* the finest American novel published in many years. Philip Rahv, in *New York Review of Books*, called it a first-rate novel . . . the best by an American writer that has appeared in some years. Edmund Fuller in the *Wall Street Journal* said that Styron without doubt is the foremost writer of his generation in American fiction. *Commentary* magazine said it is a superb novel with immense understanding. The *Los Angeles Times* called it one of the great novels by an American author in this century.

One of the mostly southern liberals working for the Southern Regional Council reviewed the novel in *New South* (Fall 1967), the Council's magazine. He found the novel richly deserving of its critical acclaim since it is an important work of fiction dealing successfully with race and the whole historical setting of slavery, one of the more important themes in American life. The reviewer defends the novel against the two critical reviews of the novel that he had seen: (1) the mild criticism of Wilfred Sheed in *The New York Times Book Review* who doubts the ability of a twentieth century white southerner like Styron to speak from the consciousness of a nineteenth century black slave and also finds technical faults in the novel; (2) H. Aptheker's charges in *The Nation* that the novel has all the rationalizations of slavery plus the slave stereotypes. The *New South* reviewer again drags out the Elkins thesis and compares the Negro slaves to the Jews in the Nazi concentration camps. But this has been refuted. (See my essay in *Freedomways*, Fall 1967). He also sidesteps Aptheker's charge of historical inaccuracy; says the novel's main achievement is its showing of the horror and cruelty of slavery. He agrees with other reviewers when they seized upon this novel and used it as an argument against today's riots. They also say that Nat's revolt prevented Virginia from solving its slavery problem. He thinks that the real moral issue today as in history is not the violence but the cause for violence.

Even James Baldwin, Styron's friend, chimes in by saying

that Styron has begun the common history—ours. And the veteran biographical and historical novelist Irving Stone, deploring the decline of what he calls the "great school of historical novelists" (*New York Times,* Jan. 19, 1968), says that *The Confessions* is the one recent historical novel that impressed him. Robert Coles, a Harvard psychiatrist, the author of the book *Children of Crisis* (1967) and the latest self-styled white "authority" on Negroes, finds Styron's psychological and historical explanations of Nat Turner completely satisfying and valid in his long, six-page review in *Partisan Review* (Winter 1968). Another high-brow magazine *Dissent* (Jan.–Feb. 1968), in its review by James MacPherson, is also favorable and uncritical in its approach to Styron's novel.

There were some dissenting reviews. Herbert Aptheker, an authority on Negro history and especially slave revolts, in addition to the short piece in *The Nation,* wrote a devastatingly critical article-review in *Political Affairs* (Oct. 1967) which we have mentioned several times. Richard Greenleaf's review of the novel in *The Worker* (Oct. 8, 1967) called it anti-Negro and a libel on Nat Turner. Another *New York Amsterdam News* columnist Gertrude Wilson wrote on Oct. 21, 1967, that Styron had done a good job in *The Confessions* and that she hoped that her column readers would read the novel; also that the novel showed that white people could understand what it is like to be black. Later she had second thoughts. In her Dec. 30, 1967, column titled "Styron's Folly," she asked: why is the book such a success among whites? She concludes that the book is so popular with whites because it proves that if Negroes retaliate against injustice by violence, they will be quelled by violence. The book also gives, she says, the blessing of history for continued violence against Negroes. Mrs. Wilson also found in Howard H. Meyer's recent biography of Thomas W. Higginson that Nat had a slave wife (with a different master from his) whom he couldn't protect at all in slavery. (There is a brief account of Nat's wife in Samuel Warner's

The Authentic and Impartial Narrative of the Tragical Scene of the Twenty Second of August, 1831 [1831].) She concludes that Styron's stereotyped picture of Nat as a celibate, as one of repressed lusts who is violently aroused by a sweet young white girl is a lie. This book is history twisted, she says, to fit the sexual fantasies of our own times.

As anyone who has read the Negro critic Albert Murray's essay "Something Different, Something More" (in Herbert Hill's *Anger and Beyond*, 1966) knows, he denounces social fiction by Negro writers which attacks our system and society and takes refuge in the art-as-mostly-technique approach to creative writing. So Murray, familiar with Styron's considerable technique in his first three novels, hoped that Styron, a so-called reconstructed southerner, would bring his fourth novel off even though he had picked a difficult subject for a white American novelist. But Murray is compelled to put *The Confessions* down and he does this in a brilliant essay-review (*The New Leader*, Dec. 4, 1967). He says that Styron failed to identify intimately with Nat Turner; that his Turner is one whom many white people will accept at a safe distance but not the hero with whom Negroes identify. Accusing Styron of building a weak Turner character according to the Elkins Sambo thesis and Freudian castration (he also calls this pro-slavery image Marxist which it isn't), he says that Styron has added a neo-Reichean hypothesis about the correlation between sex repression and revolutionary leadership; between Negro freedom from slavery and sexual desire for a white woman. Styron, he says, never realized that the Negro conception of Nat Turner as an epic hero, a special, dedicated breed of man who had given his last full measure of devotion to liberation and dignity was already geared to the dynamics of rituals and myth and hence to literature. Criticizing Styron for ignoring the many slave revolts, Murray accuses Elkins of making slavery overwhelming for Negroes but letting such a monstrous system have little effect on the whites who operated it. Murray uses Kenneth Stampp's *The Peculiar Institution* (1956) to document the great impact of the Nat Turner and other slave revolts on the slavocracy. When Styron has Nat Turner say that Negroes were bragging in brass when they said that they would kill whites, Murray replies that Negroes fought in the Revolutionary War, the War of 1812 and very bravely a little later against their Confederate slave masters in the Civil War. Describing the characters Nat Turner in *The Confessions* and the female Peyton in *Lie Down in Darkness* as having a lot of Styron's own personality in them, Murray says that if white writers want to think Negro and create Negro characters, they must be able to sing the spirituals and/or swing the blues, or, in other words, know the rugged facts and the psychological subtleties and nuances of Negro life.

Loyle Hairston did a fine critical essay-review of the novel for *Freedomways* (Winter 1968). Cecil M. Brown, a perceptive Negro critic, also did a brilliant, analytical job on Styron in his long review in *Negro Digest* (February 1968). And there are two long critical reviews of *The Confessions* by the psychologist Lloyd T. Delany and the sociologist Gerald M. Platt in the new magazine *Psychology Today* (January 1968). Platt accepts some of the false "facts" in Styron's novel and Delany calls the book a valiant and honest attempt to view the horrible institution of slavery. But Delany also calls the book Styron's confessions which are historically inaccurate, stereotyped and racist. Both Delany and Platt say that the novel presents the revolt in a vacuum with no historical context; but most important, they both show clearly and in great detail that the novel is psychologically false through and through in terms of human motivation and psychological theory and is morally wrong as well.

This novel is a good example of the absurdity of the separation of art and politics, art and sociology. This separation is nourished and encouraged by all liberal magazines such as *The New Republic, The Nation, Commentary, New York Review of Books, Dissent, Commonweal, The New Leader, The Progressive, The Reporter* and others—magazines that fight for progressive social policies and measures but take a stand-pat, art-for-art's-sake approach to fiction, plays, cinema, music and painting. Styron has lived through twelve years of the Negro social revolution and struggle in the U.S., but this upheaval has not touched him as a novelist. He wrote *The Confessions* just as he would have written it in 1948. His writing is impervious to Negro social change and struggle and to the facts of Negro history. His book is a throwback to the racist writing of the 1930's and 1940's. The decline in the writing of Styron, Ellison and many other American novelists is directly traceable to this tragic American separation of art and politics, art and sociology—as John Howard Lawson pointed out in his essay on Styron (*Mainstream*, Oct. 1960).

Sidney Finkelstein calls truthful fiction (in his book *Existentialism and Alienation* and in a review of two of Philip Stevenson's novels [*Political Affairs*, Oct. 1962]) those novels and short stories that take up the central problem of American life: that is, the conflict between the democratic principles on which the nation was founded and the forces of violence against the working people—a conflict which has been continuous throughout American history. Novelists like Stevenson, Albert Maltz, and Phillip Bonosky are attempting to help humanize U.S. human relations and extend democracy to the dispossessed even if this interferes with property and profits. This struggle, says Finkelstein further, for a more rational, realistic and truthful view of life, which includes the fight for Negro equality and rights, is a struggle for humanization of nature and social relations against alienation. The artists who depict this many-sided struggle of alienated human beings moving toward more humanization are a force in the humanization of reality. But, as Finkelstein points out, when the writers themselves are alienated and psychologically sick, as in Styron's case, their view of society and of other human beings is colored by their subjective, Freudian views of their own problems and the effect of their art is further alienation rather than humanization.

CHAPTER VII

WILLIAM STYRON'S NAT TURNER —ROGUE-NIGGER

LOYLE HAIRSTON

. . . The slave is a human being, divested of all rights,—reduced to . . . a brute . . . a mere "chattel" . . . placed beyond the circle of human brotherhood—cut off from his own kind, his name . . . In law, the slave has no wife, no children, no country, and no home. He can own nothing, possess nothing . . . but what must belong to another . . . He toils . . . [so] that another may live in idleness; he eats bolted meal so that another may eat the bread of fine flour; he rests his toil-worn limbs on the cold damp ground, that another may repose on softest pillow; he is clad in coarse and tattered raiment, that another may be arrayed in . . . fine linen; he is sheltered only by the wretched hovel, that another may dwell in a magnificent mansion; and to this condition he is bound down as by an arm of iron. . . .

—FREDERICK DOUGLASS

THE WORDS ABOVE were written by a man who himself endured twenty-one years of American slavery, before escaping to the North. But being an ex-slave, naturally, Frederick Douglass cannot be trusted to be objective and impartial. What to him was a "grand aggregation of human horrors" can be proven by men of "Christian enlightenment" to have been a system of considerable benevolence and liberality. Such is the witchcraft of the myth-makers of American history.

Reason becomes an encumbrance; logic is turned upside down in this all-out effort to conceal the motives of greed and power which characterized many of the hallowed Pilgrim Fathers. In his, *Confessions of Nat Turner*, William Styron carries this tradition to a remarkable extreme: Nat Turner's rebellion is depicted as a worse crime than slavery!

Among other things, we learn from this celebrated novel how benign the "peculiar" institution actually was; and that slaveholders were among *civilization's* most cultured and compassionate souls who endured great remorse over the role in which history had cast them.

As a service to posterity, William Styron has coerced poor Nat Turner into a full confession, proving—beyond a shadow of doubt—the vengeful ingratitude of a literate, pampered slave for his benevolent masters, an ingratitude which turns, unprovoked, into hatred and murder! After all the exquisite moralizing, this appears to be the most salient point of the novel.

But, unfortunately, William Styron does little to enlighten us on either the nobility of the human spirit or the exhausting cruelty of American slavery.

In this first-person narrative, which has Nat Turner relating the story of his life in impeccable Victorian prose, the reader is asked to believe that this sensitive, intelligent, deeply religious slave was driven to rebellion and murder solely by the fanaticism of a religious "calling." Despite some moving scenes and observations, the reader never really feels the mind of a man turned insurrectionist by the monstrous circumstances of his existence. Only in eloquent abstractions does the author permit his character to ponder the question of freedom, to dream of an existence outside the barbarity of white bondage.

Nat Turner, the literary creation, suffers the same fate as his real-life namesake: he is enslaved. He is not allowed to speak his own piece, to give expression to sentiments and passions which are born of the slave's tragic experience. This is the challenge which William Styron refused to accept as a writer.

Contrary to the "happy darky" fantasies and assorted

slave-myths, slave revolts were, in fact, frequent and numerous throughout the system's existence. The Nat Turner rebellion caused profound repercussions across the nation because the number of dead left in its wake struck a numbing fear into the hearts of slaveholders. Fifty-five members of their clan were brutally slain. Armed posses of whites and Federal troops, in turn, combed the Southampton, Virginia, area and murdered one hundred and twenty helpless slaves and "free" blacks. Nat Turner and sixteen other slaves were hanged as convicted insurrectionists. His alleged *Confession*, which was edited and published by a white southern reporter, traces the important details of the rebellion and illuminates some aspects of Nat Turner's life, keen intelligence, and his formidable character.

Apart from that *Confession* and what is left of the trial record, little is known of Nat Turner's life. William Styron's version is wholly a construction of his own considerable imagination. The writing is graceful and often moving in the lyrical beauty of many descriptive passages; but somehow it is deficient in that interior quality which is needed to breathe the illusion of life and human warmth into the work. And because of the elaborate, and sometimes heavy, style, the work seems to be more tapestry than historical literature.

But the novel fails for far more serious reasons than flaws in its form. The basic weakness must be examined in terms of the author's attitude towards his subject. When depicting black people in fiction, white writers are guilty of two fundamental faults, to which William Styron is no exception. First, they are incapable of portraying black characters as human types, and second, they look upon the black man's condition of social degradation as being natural to his *inferior* character, rather than resulting from the racial oppression of the American social system.

The lines of the contemporary stereotype have been softened with refinements like good grammar and ivy league accouterments, but Nigger Jim—whether he is Mark

Twain's simpering slave, Faulkner's obstinate Lucas Beauchamp and "matriarch" Dilsey, or William Styron's organically religious Nat Turner—remains the prototype of the white American writer's concept of the "Negro."

Indeed, it can be said with tragic certainty that, except for the contributions of black writers, modern American literature has yet to produce a convincing black character endowed with the virtues common to all mankind: the capacity for love, courage, integrity, dignity, social duty, etc.

William Styron's novel, on the surface, would seem to overcome this weakness from the way he approaches his material, particularly in form and structure. But the first-person narrative of a slave recounting the vicissitudes of his life in a very literary prose destroys whatever plausibility his Nat Turner might have had. The method has the effect of reducing the character to an abstraction, a kind of literary conduit through which the author transmits the white man's emotionally charged involvements with the black man. But with all the work's sorrowful tone, its pathos has a hollow, disquieting ring.

How can the reader become in any way emotionally involved with a character whom he feels to be a mere device?

When Nat Turner speaks, for instance, of "An exquisitely sharpened hatred for the white man" being "an emotion not difficult for Negroes to harbor," the reader is emotionally disengaged from such words coming from the mouth of a slave, however literate and articulate he might be. And there can be no reality to a slave who muses that, "this hatred does not abound in every Negro's soul; it relies upon too many mysterious and hidden patterns of life and chance to flourish luxuriantly everywhere. Real hatred . . . so pure and obdurate that no sympathy, no human warmth, no flicker of compassion can make the faintest nick . . . upon the . . . surface of its being—is not common to all Negroes. . . ."

And why is our slave so concerned about "pure" hatred? Because, in order to make good his "divine mission to kill all the white people in Southampton," he has to find a band of "Negroes in whom hatred was already ablaze" or can be cultivated. Men who would reduce fellow humans to brute-animals, in their lust for wealth and privilege, are worthy of nothing less than pure hatred. But William Styron has a different purpose in mind: by pure hatred, he is suggesting a criminal state of mind for the purpose of reducing the insurrection, in the reader's mind, to the baseness of slavery.

The emotional climax of the novel is not the description of the revolt, but the orgiastic murder of Nat Turner's master's family, rendered in vivid, bloodcurdling detail. One victim's head, "gushing blood from a matrix of pulpy crimson flesh, rolled from his neck and fell to the floor. . . . The headless body . . . slid down the wall . . . and collapsed in a pile of skinny shanks, elbows . . . *Blood deluged the room in a foaming sacrament*" [Emphasis added]. A moment later, the "blanched, hacked, bleeding corpses of Putnam and the . . . boy came clumpety-clumping down the . . . steps . . . drenching Moses's [one of Nat Turner's confederates] bare feet in vermilion." Upstairs, Hark (another executioner-confederate) cries out in a "jubilant sound" that is "oddly like music"!

Momentarily horrified by this ritualistic bloodbath in which he is soaking, Nat Turner winces in pious impotence: "Ah my God! Hast Thou truly called me to this?"

It would be far more appropriate to put the question to his literary creator. For indeed, William Styron's own "calling" has persuaded him to describe one of the most spectacular revolts against American slavery as mere wanton savagery. The brave Nat Turner's "mission" is given no broader interpretation than bloody revenge. This is thinly veiled slander, a malicious attempt to revoke his credentials as an authentic hero in mankind's struggle against tyranny. Thus, like other antislavery heroes, such as John Brown, Garrison, Lovejoy, Wendell Phillips, and Thaddeus Stevens, Nat Turner takes his proper place in the *rogues' gallery* of American history.

Such is the fate of the "Prophet" in the hands of a writer who still subscribes to the fantasy-history of an *Idyllic South,* a novelist whose ethos seems committed to the faded myths of a system that was maintained and perpetuated by the ultimate in human cruelty.

The use of the first-person device is necessary to William Styron's thematic purpose; it enables him to have Nat Turner emasculate himself as a man, as an anguished slave who—like his father before him—was driven to fatal desperation. We find the slave looking at himself, and the world around him, through the white man's distorted lenses, observing his own life with devout detachment—a kind of existentialist scorn for the *absurdities* ranging round him. His concerns are clearly not his own, but those of William Styron's homegrown concepts of what the inner life of a "Negro," a black slave, was like.

As the novel progresses, Nat Turner's character takes on those grotesque features which are so familiar and tiresome. As though bedeviled by white-supremacist-inspired fears of the black man's alleged superhuman sexual powers, William Styron triumphantly reduces his slave to a religious celibate —a kind of self-castration. Poor Nat Turner's only sexual experience is—alas!—a *homosexual* one! And guess whose image fills his sex fantasies? When masturbating, in his youth, he always envisioned himself between the legs of "a nameless white girl . . . with golden curls." There are other instances when his religious armor gives way momentarily to passions of the flesh, driving him to an uncontrollable desire to "violate" a white woman!

This is pure racism. Slaveholders themselves could not have dredged up more repugnant notions about the "nature" of black men. And since this is done in the name of art and "truth," such writing must be challenged on moral—as well as esthetic—grounds. Literature does not exist outside society and the life of man, free of responsibility and meaningful purpose. Its serious function is to illuminate something of the nature of the human condition by portraying man in the context of his reality, and the values which support his moral conventions. There is, of course, an easier alternative—to bastardize one's work by yielding to the demands of a society that lives in dread of truth.

William Styron's problem is conceptual—one of reading human history in fundamentalist terms, within the narrow confines of regional loyalty to the so-called southern tradition; a euphemism for institutional white supremacy, from its genesis in the African slave trade to modern American racism. His absorption in the Old South mystique is reminiscent of William Faulkner in tone and prose style. And like Faulkner he is able to evoke through a vivid, sensuous imagery his own emotional attitudes, philosophy, and judgments of his subject.

But for all its prose power and somber earnestness, William Styron's novel utterly fails the simple test of honesty. Moral cowardice prevents him from accepting Nat Turner as a man, as a natural member of the human family; to do so would mean to give up those illusions which bestow eminence upon *whiteness*—illusions in which his ego has so much invested.

The description of slavery quoted at the beginning of this article helps us to understand how Nat Turner, with full justification, could plead "Not guilty" at his actual trial. For can a man commit a crime against *slavery?* Only the likes of William Styron could subscribe to such a view. But in his version of Nat Turner's *Confessions,* we find the slave-rebel guilty of nothing but unwittingly exposing his author's moral senility.

Otherwise, the novel succeeds only as an eloquent forgery. For it will take more than a literary flogging to diminish the image of Nat Turner. . . .

CHAPTER VIII

OUR NAT TURNER AND WILLIAM STYRON'S CREATION

CHARLES V. HAMILTON

WILLIAM STYRON classifies his story as "a meditation on history." It is important for us, then, to view it in this sense and to see precisely what this means in terms of white America's ability or inability to come to terms with the black man in this country. This book is a best seller because it raises and treats all the problems of black people versus whites—the assertive black male, the white woman bugaboo, violence, freedom—and the ultimate treatment reinforces what white America wants to believe about black America. The treatment, in other words, turns out right for whites.

Black youth (and some not so youthful) today who are challenging the values and practices of this society, especially in regard to race, find Styron's book a prime example of the obstacles to overcome. Black youth on college campuses I visit across this country, who form black student associations and who insist on a redefinition of historical and educational legitimacy, can never and should never accept the portrayal (or is the word "betrayal"?) of Nat Turner as set forth by Styron. Granted, Styron is entitled to his literary license, but black people today cannot afford the luxury of having their leaders manipulated and toyed with. Nat Turner struck a blow for freedom; Nat Turner was a revolutionary who did *not* fail, but rather one who furthered the idea and cause of freedom precisely because he chose to act for freedom. Black people today must not permit themselves to be divested of their historical revolutionary leaders. And it is incumbent upon blacks to make this clear to the Styrons and to all those who read his book and are soothed.

We will not permit Styron's "meditation" to leave unchallenged an image of Nat Turner as a fanatical black man who dreams of going to bed with white women, who holds nothing but contempt for his fellow blacks, and who understands, somewhat, the basic human desire to be free but still believes in the basic humanity of some slaveholders.

We will not permit Styron to picture unchallenged Nat Turner as a leader who did not understand that the military defeat should not be confused with the ideological victory: i.e., a blow for freedom. The rebellion of 1831, led by Nat Turner, is important today for blacks to understand and whites to accept precisely because its lesson is that there will be leaders who *will* rise up—against all odds—to strike blows for freedom against an oppressive, inhumane system. And there can be no refuge in the thought that Turner felt himself divinely inspired or waited for signs from heaven, etc. The important thing is that the desire for human freedom resides in the black breast as well as in any other. No amount of explicating about the harshness of slavery or the gentleness of slavery, about the docility of the masses of slaves, etc. can keep that desire from exploding. Man—black or white or yellow or red—moves to maximize his freedom: THAT is the lesson of Nat Turner that Styron did not deal with.

Styron's literary mind can wander about homosexuality and the like, and his vast readership can have their stereotypes strengthened by an image of a black preacher who is irrational and weak (unable to kill, excepting some white woman he loves) and uncertain. But black people should reject this; and white people should not delude themselves.

Let us see how Styron's "meditation on history" fits perfectly with traditional, widely acclaimed historical accounts of the event and the institution of slavery. And in doing this, we will see how his book feeds the distortions of white America. I will cite two major historical texts, sources used widely in colleges and high schools. First—simply to observe the uses of history—note how Professor Thomas A. Bailey in his *The American Pageant: A History of the Republic* describes the American revolution:

> The revolutionists were blessed with outstanding leadership. Washington was a giant among men; Benjamin Franklin was a master among diplomats. . . . The Americans, in addition, enjoyed the moral advantage that came from what they regarded as a just cause. . . . The brutal truth is that only a select minority of the American colonials attached themselves to the cause of independence with a spirit of selfless devotion. These were the dedicated souls who bore the burden of battle and the risks of defeat; these were the freedom-loving patriots who deserved the gratitude and approbation of generations yet unborn. Seldom have so few done so much for so many [pp. 100–103].

Now let us see how this same objective, white American scholar deals with Nat Turner:

> Fanatical Nat Turner, a semi-educated Negro preacher who had visions, organized a conspiracy which resulted in the butchering of about sixty white Virginians, mostly women and children. The outburst was speedily crushed, but an understandable wave of hysteria swept over the South [pp. 369–370].

(When I taught at a southern Negro college, a black history professor once told me: "Oh, I always use Bailey's *American Pageant*. It is simple and clear and my students like it and find it easy to read.") To my knowledge, Professor Bailey, then on the faculty at Stanford University, is not noted for racist or anti-black views.

One other source is useful, *The American Republic* (Vol. 1, to 1865) by Richard Hofstadter, William Miller, and Daniel Aaron. Note their treatment of slavery:

The kindliest slaveholder, either as a buyer or seller, was sometimes forced to break up Negro families. In short, the slaveholder was frequently victimized by the system.

But there is a brighter side of the picture. Even some of the anti-slavery men acknowledged that ordinarily the slaves were adequately housed, clothed, and fed. The slave's diet of pork, corn-meal, molasses, and greens was coarse and monotonous, and the slave quarters were un-hygienic by modern standards. But many poor-white farm-ers lived no better. Slaves worked no longer than many northern agricultural and industrial laborers and, in areas where the "task" system was employed, a slave might com-plete his assigned chores by early afternoon and spend the rest of the day as he chose. Progressive planters en-couraged their slaves to cultivate truck gardens and keep pigs and chickens for their use or to sell. Incentive pay-ments, holidays, and entertainments alleviated the drudg-ery on some plantations, and where the work became too exacting the slaves developed their own slow-down tech-niques. House-servants found life much easier than field hands, and some gifted slaves were rewarded with posi-tions of trust and responsibility. It seems true enough that many white southerners treated their slaves affectionately and that many slaves responded to this treatment with loyalty and devotion [pp. 514–515].

Styron's novel is in this historical tradition. He does not assign to Nat Turner a basic revolutionary desire to over-come oppression. In fact, Styron clearly asserts that Turner and his followers needed specific traumatic acts to galvanize them into action: being whipped unmercifully, being sold by a "decent" owner to a tyrant, having one's wife and children taken. On the other hand, Styron joins that school of thought which believes that the kinder you treat the subjects, the more likely they are to rebel. This is related to the current notion of growing black militancy resulting from rising ex-pectations. Some of us black Americans view human bond-age as bad per se, and we believe that Nat Turner, with his basically revolutionary temperament had to strike out against that bondage. He was the real freedom-lover, the true freedom-fighter.

Styron dwells on the reason the slaves would kill those masters who were kinder to them—like Travis. This, indeed, should be a message. The focus is on the fact that they were "masters," not that they were kinder than other masters. And so the white liberal today tries to remove himself from the racism of the system, without understanding that he is part of the racist system, and those of us who are real live victims of that system cannot afford irrelevant distinctions. The white liberal feels that rhetoric and good intentions are sufficient to relieve him of responsibility. He is sadly mistaken. To him, the problem is abstract, academic. To us, it is real, tangible.

Styron imputes irony to the fact that "almost the only white man in the county who owned a truly illustrious reputation for cruelty to Negroes escaped the blade of [our] retribution." The implication being, of course, that all the violence still did not get the "right" ones, that the "good" whites suffered. And, thus, further evidence of failure. Nonsense! Then and now. The Nathaniel Francises in Styron's story exist precisely because of the support—covert or overt —of the "good white folk." No sensitive black man today confuses this point—whether Styron does or not.

It is perfectly clear why Styron's book would be a hit on the American market: it confirms white America's racist feelings. Here was an ungrateful slave, taught to read by his master, who repaid that "gift" by murder. (See what happens when you try to be a little kind to them.) Here was the fanatical black leader who held profound contempt for his own people and who led them into a senseless bloodbath destined to fail, all the while he dreamed of copulating with "Miss Anne." (They are really incapable of sticking together or of being leaders. All they really want is to have sexual intercourse with our women.) Here was the visionary who frequently doubted himself and his venture. (They are little children who really must be led and brought along slowly —for their own sake.) And, of course, here was the final act of nobility on the part of the Great White Father—Gray, the attorney—who extends the hand of forgiveness through the bars. (We must be patient and understanding with these little savages. We must show them that we are big enough to forgive.)

If this is Styron's (and white America's) "meditation on history," let the record show that this is meditation mired in misinterpretation, and that this is history many of us black people reject.

Nat Turner is our hero, unequivocally understood. He is a man who had profound respect and love for his fellow blacks and who respected black womanhood and held utter contempt for those white slavemasters who violated the purity and beauty of our black women. Nat Turner *was a success* because he perpetuated the *idea* of freedom—freedom at all cost. He will not be denied his place in the revolutionary annals of black people by white people who—through the guise of art or otherwise—feel a conscious or subconscious need to belittle him. If white America feels a need to relieve its conscience, to soften *its* confession, let it be clear that it will not be done, unchallenged, at the expense of our black brothers —past or present. That day is done. That deed is denounced.

CHAPTER IX

BACK WITH THE WIND: MR. STYRON AND THE REVEREND TURNER

MIKE THELWELL

WHEN A WORK OF FICTION is cast in the form of a novel, utilizing techniques of narrative, situation, and structure that we associate with that form, and is about an important historical event, but is defined for us as "a meditation on history" rather than a "conventional" historical novel, certain questions are forced upon us.

William Styron's *Confessions* is such a work. It straddles two genres; claims, in a sense, to transcend both; and manages to combine the problems of the two while reaping dual dividends as a "novel" which is also "history." Because the book is both "history" and a novel the public mind seems to have invested it with qualities it does not necessarily possess. The events and situations are assumed to be accurate because by being "historical" they must of necessity be "true." And as the "facts" of history are true, so, in a different sense, are the insights (read "symbolic truths") of the novel.

There can be no question that this is happening. This novel has been hailed by the white literary establishment as "revealing the agonizing essence of Negro slavery," as "a book that will make history," and one which "shows us our American past, our present, ourselves in a dazzling shaft of light." Clearly, we are in the presence of no mere "fiction" but a cultural and social document which is both "illuminating" and potentially definitive of contemporary attitudes.

In these terms certain extra-literary questions become important. Is it possible, for example, for a white southern gentleman to tune in on the impulses, beliefs, emotions, and thought-patterns of a black slave? This miracle of empathy entails an imaginative leap not only into history, but across cultures. It necessitates that writer divorcing himself from that vast mythic tradition about slavery, black people, and history which is so integral a part of his background. Then he has to devise a literary idiom through which to record his insights, since the gentleman and the slave lack common language or experience.

When black people were brought to America they were deprived of their language and of the underpinnings in cultural experience out of which a language comes. It is clear that they developed two languages, one for themselves and another for the white masters. The latter has been preserved ("parodied" is a better word) as the "Sambo" dialect in the works of southern dialect humorists—and even in Samuel Clemens at times—to whom it was often simply quaint and humorous. The only vestiges we can find of the real language of the slaves are in the few spirituals which have come down to us, which give a clue to its true tenor. It is a language produced by oppression, but one whose central impulse is survival and resistance. And it is undoubtedly the language in which Turner's rebellion and the countless other plots for insurrection were formulated. Anyone who has been privileged to catch the performance of a good black preacher in the rural South (or has heard Martin Luther King talking to a black audience) understands something of the range and flexibility of this language. Lacking complicated syntactical structure and vast vocabulary, it depends on what linguists call para-language; that is, gesture, physical expression, and modulation of cadences and intonation which serve to change the meaning—in incredibly subtle ways—of the same collection of words. It is intensely poetic and expressive, since vivid simile, creative and effective juxtaposition of images, and metaphor must serve in the absence of a large

vocabulary to cause the audience to see and feel. It is undoubtedly a language of action rather than a language of
reflection, and thus more available to the dramatist than the
novelist.

But the characterization of Nat Turner requires some literary approximation of this language. Yet Mr. Styron's Nat
speaks, or rather meditates in no language at all. His creator
places in his mouth a sterile and leaden prose that not even
massive transfusions of Old Testament rhetoric can vitalize,
a strange fusion of Latinate classicism, a kind of New England Episcopalian prissiness. At times it would seem that Mr.
Styron was trying, for whatever reason, to imitate the stodgy
"official" prose of the nineteenth-century lawyer who recorded the original confessions, at other times Nat sounds
like nothing so much as a conscious parody of the prose voice
of James Baldwin, the Negro Mr. Styron knows best, or
Faulkner at his least inspired. This is not to say that the
prose is not clear, even elegant in a baroque Victorian way,
especially in the functionally inexplicable passages of nature
writing that continuously interrupt the narrative. But, finally,
it is the language of the essay, heavy and declarative.

The language combines with the structure of the novel to
disastrous effect. Since the story begins after the fact, with
Nat already in prison reflecting on his life, much of the book
is in the form of long, unbroken monologues. Even the most
violent action or intensely felt experience seems distanced
and without immediacy, strangely lumpen.

Nat Turner operates in this novel with a "white" language
and a white consciousness. (The voice that we hear in this
novel as Turner's is that of a nineteenth-century plantation
owner. The terms in which the owner of that voice perceives
experience, and the assumptions he accepts about blacks are
colored by the racism of that class.) Since he lacks the idiom
in which Nat might communicate intimately with his peers,
Styron simply avoids the problem by having Nat spend most
of his life in that paradoxical, typically southern situation,

close to but isolated from whites. This isolation in proximity becomes his obsession. And as his language is "white," so are his values and desires. Styron's Nat Turner, the house nigger, is certainly not the emotional or psychological prototype of the rebellious slave: he is the spiritual ancestor of the contemporary middle-class Negro, that is to say the Negro type with whom whites including Mr. Styron feel most comfortable.

Conspicuously intelligent—in their terms—Nat aspires hopelessly to the culture and stature of his white masters. Naturally (in his master's terms), he holds in contempt the society of his own people whom he considers dumb, mindless, unsalvageable brutes unfitted either for freedom or salvation. Hating the blackness which limits the possibilities which he feels should be his by right of intelligence and accomplishment, he becomes a schizoid nigger-baiter. What this Nat Turner really wants is to become white, and, failing that, to integrate. As a type this Nat certainly exists *today;* 1831 is a different question. There is nothing in the historical record to justify such a characterization of Turner.

The primary historical source, Gray's *Confessions of Nat Turner,* is extremely brief, about 4,000 words. What emerges there is that Nat's character and attitudes in his formative years were influenced by his family (his father, mother, and grandmother, with whom he was very close) and the slave society. He becomes a leader and a plotter very early, and organizes his black brothers in the clandestine resistance of slavery symbolized by stealing. Later he becomes a preacher, that is a leader and a minister among the slaves. When he stops fraternizing with his peers it is not out of any disdain or contempt, but for the very good political reason that "Having soon discovered to be great, I must appear so, and therefore studiously avoided mixing in society, and wrapped myself in mystery, . . ."

In Mr. Styron's novel Nat's formative years are somewhat different. He has no knowledge of his father. His grand-

mother, a mute, catatonic, culturally shocked Coromantee
wench, barely survives to give birth to his mother after dis-
embarking from the slave ship. But Nat's master, who is
mentioned only once in the Gray text, and then it is stated
only that he was "religious," is elevated by Styron to be the
major influence on Nat's early life. Discovering Nat with a
book stolen from his library (an occasion of great surprise
since no nigger ever expressed interest in literacy) he has Nat
tutored by his own daughter. Nat becomes a favorite, does
light work around the great house, and observes the ele-
gance, enlightenment, and moral superiority of his owners
and strives to emulate and impress them. He feels superior to
all other "niggers." Of his kindly and benevolent master Nat
reports: ". . . I hold him in such awe, that I am forced to
regard him, physically as well as spiritually, in terms of the
same patriarchal and venerable grandeur that glows forth
from . . . Moses on the mount, . . ." Such "awe" indeed
that, in his own rather than Styron's version, he is leading his
fellows in raids on the venerable patriarch's property!

Marse Samuel does in due course reveal to Nat that having
educated him, he intends to free him. This contingency terri-
fies Styron's Nat who knows only one free black man. The
wise and kindly master has however anticipated his in-
security and reassures Nat that he has devised a method to
give him his freedom gradually. Nat is satisfied. (No explanation is given in the novel of the process by which Nat moves
from this abject dependence to the self-confidence that al-
lows him to accept responsibility for a colony of free rebels
that it was his intention to found in the Dismal Swamp.)

This response (Please, good Massa, dis yer Darkie ain't
studyin' no freedom) is, of course, one of the favorite clichés
of a certain school of plantation melodrama. Its inclusion
here violates the historical evidence. This is not to say that
it had no basis in reality, but that there were other realities
which are not shown. In order to make Nat's response cred-
ible (remember he is the most intelligent and enlightened of

any slave shown) Styron includes an image of "The Freed Slave," who is starving, confused, and totally incapable of surviving. This is misleading, since the fact is that there were free blacks in every southern community, at times whole colonies of them, who worked in many instances as skilled artisans, and some of whom, to their discredit, even owned slaves. In 1831 there were in Southampton county 1,746 free blacks many of whom owned land. What is important here is that both slave masters and slaves knew this, and, for the slaves, these free Negroes represented a constant inspiration.

The figure of Marse Samuel is familiar: a landed Virginia gentleman, for whom slavery is not a financial operation, but the exercise of a moral obligation. His home, to which the First Families of Virginia, "with names like Byrd and Clark" traveled gathered in elaborate carriages, rivals Tara in its gentility, charm, and benevolence. This is the golden age of southern chivalry, and what is being reconstructed for us is the enlightened benevolence of the "Old Dominion" version of slavery, surely the least oppressive serfdom in mankind's history. It applies only, as Mr. Styron is careful to indicate, to slaves fortunate enough to be owned by the enlightened gentry; it is the poor white overseers and small landholders who made the lot of slaves unendurable. But we do know that it is precisely on these large Virginia plantations that the most degrading and debasing form of slavery was developed. Even as early as the 1830's, the Virginia land being increasingly exhausted by tobacco, these enlightened aristocrats had begun converting their plantations to breeding farms— that is to say, to breeding black men and women like animals for the purpose of supplying the labor markets of the Deep South. That's one reality which is only fleetingly mentioned in this novel.[1]

But in the great house Nat becomes "a pet, . . . the little

---

[1] In 1837 the Old Dominion exported to the death camps of the Deep South 40,000 black bodies for a net income of twenty-four million dollars.

black jewel of Turner's Mill. Pampered, fondled, nudged, pinched, I was the household's spoiled child, . . ." Enjoying great leisure he can lurk around for "a rare glimpse, face to face, of the pure, proud, astonishing, smooth-skinned beauty. . . ." of Miss Emmaline, she who moved with ". . . a proud serenity . . . which was pure and good in itself, like the disembodied, transparent beauty of an imagined angel," worshiping her with a "virginal" passion. Imagine then, his trauma when he finds her rutting with her cousin on the lawn and, in her passion, blaspheming God's name.

For Nat, the experience, shattering as we are asked to believe it is, constitutes a form of emancipation. He had long rejected as too common the idea of sex with black wenches and substituted for it onanistic fantasies with faceless white women. After his "angel's" fall from grace, he says, ". . . in my fantasies she began to replace the innocent, imaginary girl with the golden curls as the object of my craving, . . . and . . . allowed me to partake of the wicked and godless yet unutterable joys of defilement." Nat becomes an inverted, frustrated, onanistic, emotionally short-circuited lecher after white women. Presumably, if he had given way to his secret lust and raped the white girl he is later to murder, the rebellion would never have occurred. This Freud, moonlight, and magnolia view of history is presented as the basic motivation for the rebellion. Even if it did not come dangerously close to reiterating the infuriating sexual slander of the Negro male that is the stock-in-trade of the American racist, desire turned malignant in frustration would be as unacceptable as a theory of Turner's motives, since this kind of neurotic frustration finds expression in solitary, suicidal acts of violence, not in planned, public, political acts of rebellion.

In Gray's *Confessions* Nat Turner tells us that as he grew to young manhood the memory of what had been said about him as a child by "white and black" that he was too spirited to be a tractable slave began to obsess him, "finding I

had arrived to man's estate and was a slave." But he says
he is consoled by the spirit of prophecy which indicates to
him that there is a preordained role for him in that position.
He begins his ministry and continually exhorts his people
who "believed and said my wisdom came from God." That
he is a man of charisma and magnetism is evident. He seems
totally preoccupied with his God and his people and the
only mention of any white person at this time is of an overseer from whom he runs away. Nat is at large for thirty days,
and then returns voluntarily because the Spirit orders him
to return to his "mission," the exact nature of which he does
not yet know. Upon his return the Negroes were astonished
—"and murmured against me, saying that if they had my
sense they would not serve any master in the world." This is,
significantly, one of the few cases on record of any slave
returning voluntarily to slavery. What did it mean?

Nat's stated reason for returning must stand as a masterpiece of irony. He simply quotes one of the Biblical texts
best loved by slave owners, "he who knoweth his Master's
will, and doeth it not, shall be beaten with many stripes,
and thus have I chastened you." To the slave master this
must have been gratifying indeed, evidence further of the
faithful darky, well-steeped in the acceptable slave morality.
To Nat, knowing that his master is God, a terrible, vengeful
God, who has selected him for a "mission," it meant quite
something else. He may even have undertaken the escape
simply to establish his trustworthiness, thereby getting the
mobility necessary to organize.

Let us examine how Styron's omission of this incident
serves the "interpretation" presented in his novel. While the
historical Turner is trying to regain the confidence of his
fellows, who are angry, incredulous, and suspicious at the
idea of a man returning voluntarily to slavery, Styron's Nat
Turner is fuming and fulminating endlessly at the spiritless
servility of his fellow slaves, who are presented as totally
lacking in the will or imagination to change their condition.
There can be no question that "Uncle Toms" existed, but it

is also equally clear that they and the attitudes they represented were seized upon by slavery's apologists and publicized and exaggerated out of all proportion, while militance
and rebelliousness were played down. Who can doubt this
after hearing any contemporary southern sheriff mouthing
his eternal platitude, "our niggers are happy."

The reality of slavery[2] was that the slaves were constantly
resisting and rebelling, whether by sabotage, malingering, escape to the North, physical retaliation to attack, plotting insurrection (with a frequency that caused the masters to live in
a state of constant apprehension and under conditions of con-
tinual vigilance and security), running off to join Indian
tribes, or forming small bands of armed guerillas operating
out of swamps and remote areas. It is difficult to imagine
why, if the majority of slaves were inert "Sambos," broken
in mind and spirit, as Styron's Nat suggests, southern gov-
ernors have filled the official record with so many requests
for federal troops to guard against insurrection.

Two further examples of incidents reported in the original
Confessions and transformed by Mr. Styron's imagination are
indicative of the pattern of interpretation throughout the
book. Turner tells of converting and baptizing a white man,
an event unprecedented in Tidewater Virginia of the time,
and one which would probably cause an equally great furor
were it to happen today. The two men are refused access to
the church and repair to the river for the ceremony, where
they are mocked and threatened by a white crowd.

In Styron's version, the white convert is a drunken, de-
generate, child-molesting pederast, and is shown as a type—
the subhuman, white trash "cracker"—that one finds in the
works of writers like Erskine Caldwell. As in the omission
of Nat's voluntary return, the logic dictating such an interpretation is not clear, but this is how the only white who
is shown associating with slaves on anything that looks like
simple human terms is presented.

[2] By testimony of the slaves themselves. See *A Folk History of
Slavery*, B. A. Bodkin, Ed.

Another instance of arbitrary and derogatory "interpretation" concerns a slave called Will, who invited himself to join the insurrection. He is different from the other conspirators in that he does not have to be recruited, he volunteers. In the original *Confession,* Turner reports finding Will among his men when he joins them on the day of the insurrection: "I . . . asked Will how came he there, he answered, his life was worth no more than others, and his liberty as dear [to him.] I asked him if he thought to obtain it? He said he would, or lose his life. This was enough to put him in full confidence." In the subsequent violence Will is identified specifically as "dispatching" a number of people, while most of the other murders are not attributed to members of the band. The most that can be said of Turner's references to Will is that they show him operating with a single-minded efficiency in carrying out the work at hand. In the context of Turner's narrative there is no suggestion of dementia or frenzy in Will's actions. Like Joshua he is simply engaged in the destruction of the Lord's enemies.

In the novel, Styron's Nat sees "the demented, . . . hate-ravished, mashed-in face . . ." of Will, whose "woolly head was filled with cockleburs. A scar glistened on his black cheek, shiny as an eel cast up on a mud bank. I felt that if I reached out I could almost touch with my fingertips the madness stirring within him, feel a shaggy brute heaving beneath the carapace of a black skin." Will is "streaked with mud, stinking, fangs bared beneath a nose stepped upon and bent like a flattened spoon, . . ." His eyes shine with a "malign fire" and he bears a hatred toward "all mankind, all creation." We learn that Will has been reduced to this condition of bestiality by the unendurable cruelties of a sadistic master so that his is not the "natural depravity" that another generation of southern writers would have evoked. But even so, this portrait of an evolutionary marvel, half-nigger, half-beast, is surely familiar to anyone who knows such classics of southern literature as Dixon's *The Klansman.* His has been a long history and I had hoped that having served his time on the pages of southern fiction this particular stereotype could now be laid to rest. It is saddening to see the poor fellow resurrected by a writer of Mr. Styron's unquestioned sophistication. As he sidles into the scene, stinking and licking his fangs, we recognize his function: he will rape a white woman. And thirty pages later, despite Nat's injunctions against rape (no sexual incidents are mentioned in the record of the trial), an injunction all the nobler in light of his own perennial, frustrated cravings, we find this scene:

> "There deserted of all save those two acting out their final tableau—the tar-black man and the woman, bone-white, bone-rigid with fear beyond telling, pressed urgently together against the door in a simulacrum of shattered oneness and heartsick farewell . . ."

and it looks as if nigger-beast has struck again.[3]

[3] James Wells Brown, a Negro, whose book on the Negro in the American Revolution appeared in 1867, mentions the Nat Turner rebellion. His version does not in any way contradict the meager court record that is the original *Confessions*, but it adds information not included. One may speculate as to the source of this information—possibly newspaper accounts of the time, or the testimony of black survivors of the incident—but the account is of interest, representing, as it does, an early account of the insurrection, by a black man. About Will, Brown has this to say:

> Among those who joined the conspirators was Will, a slave who scorned the idea of taking his master's name. Though his soul longed to be free, he evidently became one of the party as much to satisfy revenge as for the liberty he saw in the dim future . . . His own back was covered with scars from his shoulders to his feet. A large scar running from his right eye down to his chin showed that he had lived with a cruel master. Nearly six feet in height and one of the strongest and most athletic of his race, he proved to be one of the most unfeeling of the insurrectionists. His only weapon was a broad axe, sharp and heavy.

Brown then quotes, from the original *Confessions*, Will's path of carnage, and next describes his death in the final skirmish.

> In this battle there were many slain on both sides. Will, the bloodthirsty and revengeful slave, fell with his broad axe uplifted, after

There is, finally, the major invention that gives color to the entire novel. Mr. Styron, contrary to any historical evidence, has Turner's ultimate defeat coming as a result of the actions of loyal slaves who fought in defense of their beloved masters. That these slaves are identified as "owned by the gentry" further underlines the book's emphasis on the benign nature of "aristocratic slavery," which was able to command the loyalty of these slaves who were, in one white character's words, "living too well."

This thing which did not happen is made into one of the central motifs of the book. Turner broods on the memory of "Negroes in great numbers . . . firing back at us with as much passion and fury and *even* skill as their white owners . . ." When his lieutenant, Hark, falls, Turner recalls "three bare-chested Negroes . . . in the pantaloons of *coachmen* . . . kick him back to earth with booted feet. Hark flopped around in desperation, but they kicked him again, kicked him with an exuberance not caused by any white man's urging or threat or exhortation but with rackety glee, . . ." [Emphasis added]. And so, dispirited and broken, Nat sits in his cell feeling himself betrayed by his people and his God: "It seemed . . . that my black shit-eating people were surely like flies, God's mindless outcasts, lacking even that will to destroy by their own hand their unending anguish . . ."[4]

---

having laid three of the whites dead at his feet with his own strong arm and terrible weapon. His last words were, "Bury my axe with me." For he religiously believed that, in the next world, the blacks would have a contest with the whites, and he would need his axe.

No sociological comment is necessary. But from a purely literary standpoint, it should be clear that Will, lifelong rebel and archetypal destroyer, presents possibilities which Mr. Styron simply ignored in favor of the "ravening, incoherent black beast" stereotype.

[4] Brown's version makes it clear, as do the court records, that Turner's defeat came at the hands of whites. No black loyalist mercenaries are mentioned, but he does give an instance of a master's life being saved by a slave. That, too, is instructive:

In the original *Confessions* he shows no such uncertainty or bitterness. When asked if he could not see that the entire undertaking was a mistake, he answers simply, "Was not Christ crucified?" Gray's final description of him is significant . . . ". . . clothed with rags and covered with chains: yet daring to raise his manacled hands to heaven, with a spirit soaring above the attributes of man; I looked on him and my blood curdled in my veins."

If this book is important, it is so not because it tells much about Negro experience during slavery but because of the manner in which it demonstrates the persistence of white southern myths, racial stereotypes, and literary clichés even in the best intentioned and most enlightened minds. Their largely uncritical acceptance in literary circles shows us how far we still have to go. The real "history" of Nat Turner, and indeed of black people, remains to be written.

On the fatal night, when Nat and his companions were dealing death to all they found, Capt. Harris, a wealthy planter, had his life saved by the devotion and timely warning of his slave Jim, said to have been half brother to his master. After the revolt had been put down, and parties of whites were out hunting the suspected blacks, Capt. Harris with his faithful slave went into the woods in search of the Negroes. In saving his master's life Jim felt he had done his duty, and could not consent to become a betrayer of his race; and, on reaching the woods, he handed his pistol to his master, and said, "I cannot help you hunt down these men: they, like myself, want to be free. Sir, I am tired of the life of a slave: please give me my freedom or shoot me on the spot." Capt. Harris took the weapon, and pointed at the slave . . . The Capt. fired and the slave fell dead at his feet.

I do not claim that this incident necessarily took place in exactly the way that Brown relates it. But it also seems too specific to be pure invention on the part of Mr. Brown, who was, after all, writing history and not fiction. It seems most probable that this was one of those minor incidents which become part of the folk lore surrounding any major event; it is discussed, passed on, almost certainly distorted in the telling, but for some reason not included in "official" records. In this case, moreover, the nature of the incident suggests a reason for its exclusion.

THE

CONFESSIONS

OF

NAT TURNER,

THE LEADER OF THE LATE

INSURRECTION IN SOUTHAMPTON, VA.

As fully and voluntarily made to

THOMAS R. GRAY,

In the prison where he was confined, and acknowledged by
him to be such when read before the Court of Southampton; with the certificate, under seal of
the Court convened at Jerusalem,
Nov. 5, 1831, for his trial.

ALSO, AN AUTHENTIC

ACCOUNT OF THE WHOLE INSURRECTION,

WITH LISTS OF THE WHITES WHO WERE MURDERED,

AND OF THE NEGROES BROUGHT BEFORE THE COURT OF
SOUTHAMPTON, AND THERE SENTENCED, &c.

Baltimore:

PUBLISHED BY THOMAS R. GRAY.
Lucas & Deaver, print.
1831.

THE TEXT OF

THE CONFESSIONS OF NAT TURNER . . .

AS REPORTED BY THOMAS R. GRAY

(1831)

DISTRICT OF COLUMBIA, TO WIT:

Be it remembered, That on this tenth day of November, Anno Domini, eighteen hundred and thirty-one, Thomas R. Gray of the said District, deposited in this office the title of a book, which is in the words as following:

"The Confessions of Nat Turner, the leader of the late insurrection in Southampton, Virginia, as fully and voluntarily made to Thomas R. Gray, in the prison where he was confined, and acknowledged by him to be such when read before the Court of Southampton; with the certificate, under seal, of the Court convened at Jerusalem, November 5, 1831, for his trial. Also, an authentic account of the whole insurrection, and with lists of the whites who were murdered, and of the negroes brought before the Court of Southampton, and there sentenced, &. the right whereof he claims as proprietor, in conformity with an Act of Congress, entitled "An act to amend the several acts respecting Copy Rights."

EDMUND J. LEE, Clerk of the District. In testimony that the above is a true copy, from the record of the District Court for the District of Columbia, I, [Seal.]   Edmund J. Lee, the Clerk thereof, have hereunto set my hand and affixed the seal of my office, this 10th day of November, 1831.

EDMUND J. LEE, C. D. C.

TO THE PUBLIC

The late insurrection in Southampton has greatly excited
the public mind, and led to a thousand idle, exaggerated
and mischievous reports. It is the first instance in our history
of an open rebellion of the slaves, and attended with such
atrocious circumstances of cruelty and destruction, as could
not fail to leave a deep impression, not only upon the minds
of the community where this fearful tragedy was wrought,
but throughout every portion of our country, in which this
population is to be found. Public curiosity has been on the
stretch to understand the origin and progress of this dreadful
conspiracy, and the motives which influence its diabolical
actors. The insurgent slaves had all been destroyed, or apprehended, tried and executed, (with the exception of the
leader,) without revealing any thing at all satisfactory, as
to the motives which governed them, or the means by which
they expected to accomplish their object. Every thing con-
nected with the sad affair was wrapt in mystery, until Nat
Turner, the leader of this ferocious band, whose name has
resounded throughout our widely extended empire, was
captured. This "great Bandit" was taken by a single individual, in a cave near the residence of his late owner, on
Sunday, the thirtieth of October, without attempting to make
the slightest resistance, and on the following day safely
lodged in the jail of the County. His captor was Benjamin
Phipps, armed with a shot gun well charged. Nat's only
weapon was a small light sword which he immediately sur-
rendered, and begged that his life might be spared. Since
his confinement, by permission of the Jailor, I have had
ready access to him, and finding that he was willing to make
a full and free confession of the origin, progress and con-
summation of the insurrectory movements of the slaves of
which he was the contriver and head; I determined for the

gratification of public curiosity to commit his statements to writing, and publish them, with little or no variation, from his own words. That this is a faithful record of his confessions, the annexed certificate of the County Court of Southampton, will attest. They certainly bear one stamp of truth and sincerity. He makes no attempt (as all the other insurgents who were examined did,) to exculpate himself, but frankly acknowledges his full participation in all the guilt of the transaction. He was not only the contriver of the conspiracy, but gave the first blow towards its execution.

It will thus appear, that whilst every thing upon the surface of society wore a calm and peaceful aspect; whilst not one note of preparation was heard to warn the devoted inhabitants of woe and death, a gloomy fanatic was revolving in the recesses of his own dark, bewildered, and overwrought mind, schemes of indiscriminate massacre to the whites. Schemes too fearfully executed as far as his fiendish band proceeded in their desolating march. No cry for mercy penetrated their flinty bosoms. No acts of remembered kindness made the least impression upon these remorseless murderers. Men, women and children, from hoary age to helpless infancy were involved in the same cruel fate. Never did a band of savages do their work of death more unsparingly. Apprehension for their own personal safety seems to have been the only principle of restraint in the whole course of their bloody proceedings. And it is not the least remarkable feature in this horrid transaction, that a band actuated by such hellish purposes, should have resisted so feebly, when met by the whites in arms. Desperation alone, one would think, might have led to greater efforts. More than twenty of them attacked Dr. Blunt's house on Tuesday morning, a little before day-break, defended by two men and three boys. They fled precipitately at the first fire; and their future plans of mischief, were entirely disconcerted and broken up. Escaping thence, each individual sought his own safety either in concealment, or by returning home, with the hope that his participation might escape detection, and all were shot down in the course of a few days, or captured and brought to trial and punishment. Nat has survived all his followers, and the gallows will speedily close his career. His own account of the conspiracy is submitted to the public, without comment. It reads an awful, and it is hoped, a useful lesson, as to the operations of a mind like his, endeavoring to grapple with things beyond its reach. How it first became bewildered and confounded, and finally corrupted and led to the conception and perpetration of the most atrocious and heart-rending deeds. It is calculated also to demonstrate the policy of our laws in restraint of this class of our population, and to induce all those entrusted with their execution, as well as our citizens generally, to see that they are strictly and rigidly enforced. Each particular community should look to its own safety, whilst the general guardians of the laws, keep a watchful eye over all. If Nat's statements can be relied on, the insurrection in this county was entirely local, and his designs confided but to a few, and these in his immediate vicinity. It was not instigated by motives of revenge or sudden anger, but the results of long deliberation, and a settled purpose of mind. The offspring of gloomy fanaticism, acting upon materials but too well prepared for such impressions. It will be long remembered in the annals of our country, and many a mother as she presses her infant darling to her bosom, will shudder at the recollection of Nat Turner, and his band of ferocious miscreants.

Believing the following narrative, by removing doubts and conjectures from the public mind which otherwise must have remained, would give general satisfaction, it is respectfully submitted to the public by their ob't serv't,

T. R. GRAY

Jerusalem, Southampton, Va. Nov. 5, 1831.

We the undersigned, members of the Court convened at Jerusalem, on Saturday, the 5th day of Nov. 1831, for the trial of Nat, *alias* Nat Turner, a negro slave, late the property of Putnam Moore, deceased, do hereby certify, that the confessions of Nat, to Thomas R. Gray, was read to him in our presence, and that Nat acknowledged the same to be full, free, and voluntary; and that furthermore, when called upon by the presiding Magistrate of the Court, to state if he had any thing to say, why sentence of death should not be passed upon him, replied he had nothing further than he had communicated to Mr. Gray. Given under our hands and seals at Jerusalem, this 5th day of November, 1831.

JEREMIAH COBB,	[Seal.]
THOMAS PRETLOW,	[Seal.]
JAMES W. PARKER,	[Seal.]
CARR BOWERS,	[Seal.]
SAMUEL B. HINES,	[Seal.]
ORRIS A. BROWNE,	[Seal.]

State of Virginia, Southampton County, to wit:

I, James Rochelle, Clerk of the County Court of Southampton in the State of Virginia, do hereby certify, that Jeremiah Cobb, Thomas Pretlow, James W. Parker, Carr Bowers, Samuel B. Hines, and Orris A. Browne, esqr's are acting Justices of the Peace, in and for the County aforesaid, and were members of the Court which convened at Jerusalem, on Saturday the 5th day of November, 1831, for the trial of Nat *alias* Nat Turner, a negro slave, late the property of Putnam Moore, deceased, who was tried and convicted, as an insurgent in the late insurrection in the county of Southampton aforesaid, and that full faith and credit are due, and ought to be given to their acts as Justices of the peace aforesaid.

[Seal.]   In testimony whereof, I have hereunto set my hand and caused the seal of the Court aforesaid, to be affixed this 5th day of November, 1831

JAMES ROCHELLE,

C. S. C. C.

CONFESSION

Agreeable to his own appointment, on the evening he was committed to prison, with permission of the jailer, I visited NAT on Tuesday the 1st November, when, without being questioned at all, he commenced his narrative in the following words:—

SIR,—You have asked me to give a history of the motives which induced me to undertake the late insurrection, as you call it—To do so I must go back to the days of my infancy, and even before I was born. I was thirty-one years of age the 2nd of October last, and born the property of Benj. Turner, of this county. In my childhood a circumstance occurred which made an indelible impression on my mind, and laid the ground work of that enthusiasm, which has terminated so fatally to many, both white and black, and for which I am about to atone at the gallows. It is here necessary to relate this circumstance—trifling as it may seem, it was the commencement of that belief which has grown with time, and even now, sir, in this dungeon, helpless and forsaken as I am, I cannot divest myself of. Being at play with other children, when three or four years old, I was telling them something, which my mother overhearing, said it had happened before I was born—I stuck to my story, however, and related somethings which went, in her opinion, to confirm it—others being called on were greatly astonished, knowing that these things had happened, and caused them to say in my hearing, I surely would be a prophet, as the Lord had shewn me things that had happened before my birth. And my father and mother strengthened me in this my first impression, saying in my presence, I was intended for some great purpose, which they had always thought from certain marks on my head and breast—[a parcel of excrescences which I believe are not at all uncommon, particularly among negroes, as I have seen several with the same. In this case he has either cut them off or they have nearly disappeared]—My grandmother, who was very religious, and to whom I was much attached—my master, who belonged to the church, and other religious persons who visited the house, and whom I often saw at prayers, noticing the singularity of my manners, I suppose, and my uncommon intelligence for a child, remarked I had too much sense to be raised, and if I was, I would never be of any service to any one as a slave—To a mind like mine, restless, inquisitive and observant of every thing that was passing, it is easy to suppose that religion was the subject to which it would be directed, and although this subject principally occupied my thoughts—there was nothing that I saw or heard of to which my attention was not directed—The manner in which I learned to read and write, not only had great influence on my own mind, as I acquired it with the most perfect ease, so much so, that I have no recollection whatever of learning the alphabet—but to the astonishment of the family, one day, when a book was shewn to me to keep me from crying, I began spelling the names of different objects—this was a source of wonder to all in the neighborhood, particularly the blacks—and this learning was constantly improved at all opportunities—when I got large enough to go to work, while employed, I was reflecting on many things that would present themselves to my imagination, and whenever an opportunity occurred of looking at a book, when the school children were getting their lessons, I would find many things that the fertility of my own imagination had depicted to me before; all my time, not devoted to my master's service, was spent either in prayer, or in making experiments in casting different things in moulds made of earth, in attempting to make paper, gun-powder, and many other experiments, that although I could not perfect, yet convinced me of its practicability if I had the means.° I was not addicted to stealing in

° When questioned as to the manner of manufacturing those different articles, he was found well informed on the subject.

my youth, nor have ever been—Yet such was the confidence
of the negroes in the neighborhood, even at this early period
of my life, in my superior judgment, that they would often
carry me with them when they were going on any roguery,
to plan for them. Growing up among them, with this confidence in my superior judgment, and when this, in their
opinions, was perfected by Divine inspiration, from the
circumstances already alluded to in my infancy, and which
belief was ever afterwards zealously inculcated by the
austerity of my life and manners, which became the subject
of remark by white and black.—Having soon discovered to
be great, I must appear so, and therefore studiously avoided
mixing in society, and wrapped myself in mystery, devoting
my time to fasting and prayer—By this time, having arrived
to man's estate, and hearing the scriptures commented on
at meetings, I was struck with that particular passage which
says: "Seek ye the kingdom of Heaven and all things shall
be added unto you." I reflected much on this passage, and
prayed daily for light on this subject—As I was praying one
day at my plough, the spirit spoke to me, saying "Seek ye
the kingdom of Heaven and all things shall be added unto
you." *Question*—what do you mean by the Spirit. *Ans.* The
Spirit that spoke to the prophets in former days—and I was
greatly astonished, and for two years prayed continually,
whenever my duty would permit—and then again I had the
same revelation, which fully confirmed me in the impression
that I was ordained for some great purpose in the hands of
the Almighty. Several years rolled round, in which many
events occurred to strengthen me in this my belief. At this
time I reverted in my mind to the remarks made of me in my
childhood, and the things that had been shewn me—and as it
had been said of me in my childhood by those by whom I
had been taught to pray, both white and black, and in whom
I had the greatest confidence, that I had too much sense to
be raised, and if I was, I would never be of any use to any
one as a slave. Now finding I had arrived to man's estate, and
was a slave, and these revelations being made known to me,

I began to direct my attention to this great object, to fulfil the purpose for which, by this time, I felt assured I was intended. Knowing the influence I had obtained over the minds of my fellow servants, (not by the means of conjuring and such like tricks—for to them I always spoke of such things with contempt) but by the communion of the Spirit whose revelations I often communicated to them, and they believed and said my wisdom came from God. I now began to prepare them for my purpose, by telling them something was about to happen that would terminate in fulfilling the great promise that had been made to me—About this time I was placed under an overseer, from whom I ranaway—and after remaining in the woods thirty days, I returned, to the astonishment of the negroes on the plantation, who thought I had made my escape to some other part of the country, as my father had done before. But the reason of my return was, that the Spirit appeared to me and said I had my wishes directed to the things of this world, and not to the kingdom of Heaven, and that I should return to the service of my earthly master—"For he who knoweth his Master's will, and doeth it not, shall be beaten with many stripes, and thus have I chastened you." And the negroes found fault, and murmured against me, saying that if they had my sense they would not serve any master in the world. And about this time I had a vision—and I saw white spirits and black spirits engaged in battle, and the sun was darkened—the thunder rolled in the Heavens, and blood flowed in streams—and I heard a voice saying, "Such is your luck, such you are called to see, and let it come rough or smooth, you must surely bare it." I now withdrew myself as much as my situation would permit, from the intercourse of my fellow servants, for the avowed purpose of serving the Spirit more fully—and it appeared to me, and reminded me of the things it had already shown me, and that it would then reveal to me the knowledge of the elements, the revolution of the planets, the operation of tides, and changes of the seasons. After this revelation in the year of 1825, and the knowledge of the elements being made known to me, I sought more than ever to obtain true holiness before the great day of judgment should appear, and then I began to receive the true knowledge of faith. And from the first steps of righteousness until the last, was I made perfect; and the Holy Ghost was with me, and said, "Behold me as I stand in the Heavens"—and I looked and saw the forms of men in different attitudes—and there were lights in the sky to which the children of darkness gave other names than what they really were—for they were the lights of the Savior's hands, stretched forth from east to west, even as they were extended on the cross on Calvary for the redemption of sinners. And I wondered greatly at these miracles, and prayed to be informed of a certainty of the meaning thereof—and shortly afterwards, while laboring in the field, I discovered drops of blood on the corn as though it were dew from heaven—and I communicated it to many, both white and black, in the neighborhood—and I then found on the leaves in the woods hieroglyphic characters, and numbers, with the forms of men in different attitudes, portrayed in blood, and representing the figures I had seen before in the heavens. And now the Holy Ghost had revealed itself to me, and made plain the miracles it had shown me—For as the blood of Christ had been shed on this earth, and had ascended to heaven for the salvation of sinners, and was now returning to earth again in the form of dew—and as the leaves on the trees bore the impression of the figures I had seen in the heavens, it was plain to me that the Savior was about to lay down the yoke he had borne for the sins of men, and the great day of judgment was at hand. About this time I told these things to a white man, (Etheldred T. Brantley) on whom it had a wonderful effect—and he ceased from his wickedness, and was attacked immediately with a cutaneous eruption, and blood oozed from the pores of his skin, and after praying and fasting nine days, he was healed, and the Spirit appeared to me again, and said, as the Savior had been baptised so should we be also—and when the white people would not let us be baptised by the church, we went down into the water together, in the sight of many who reviled us, and were baptised by the Spirit—After this I rejoiced greatly, and gave thanks to God. And on the 12th of May, 1828, I heard a loud noise in the heavens, and the Spirit instantly appeared to me and said the Serpent was loosened, and Christ had laid down the yoke he had borne for the sins of men, and that I should take it on and fight against the Serpent, for the time was fast approaching when the first should be last and the last should be first. *Ques.* Do you not find yourself mistaken now? *Ans.* Was not Christ crucified? And by signs in the heavens that it would make known to me when I should commence the great work—and until the first sign appeared, I should conceal it from the knowledge of men—And on the appearance of the sign, (the eclipse of the sun last February) I should arise and prepare myself, and slay my enemies with their own weapons. And immediately on the sign appearing in the heavens, the seal was removed from my lips, and I communicated the great work laid out for me to do, to four in whom I had the greatest confidence, (Henry, Hark, Nelson, and Sam)—It was intended by us to have begun the work of death on the 4th July last— Many were the plans formed and rejected by us, and it affected my mind to such a degree, that I fell sick, and the time passed without our coming to any determination how to commence—Still forming new schemes and rejecting them, when the sign appeared again, which determined me not to wait longer.

Since the commencement of 1830, I had been living with Mr. Joseph Travis, who was to me a kind master, and placed the greatest confidence in me; in fact, I had no cause to complain of his treatment to me. On Saturday evening, the 20th of August, it was agreed between Henry, Hark and myself, to prepare a dinner the next day for the men we expected, and then to concert a plan, as we had not yet determined on any. Hark, on the following morning, brought a pig, and Henry brandy, and being joined by Sam, Nelson, Will and Jack, they prepared in the woods a dinner, where, about three o'clock, I joined them.

Q. Why were you so backward in joining them.

A. The same reason that had caused me not to mix with them for years before.

I saluted them on coming up, and asked Will how came he there, he answered, his life was worth no more than others, and his liberty as dear to him. I asked him if he thought to obtain it? He said he would, or lose his life. This was enough to put him in full confidence. Jack, I knew, was only a tool in the hands of Hark, it was quickly agreed we should commence at home (Mr. J. Travis') on that night, and until we had armed and equipped ourselves, and gathered sufficient force, neither age nor sex was to be spared, (which was invariably adhered to). We remained at the feast, until about two hours in the night, when we went to the house and found Austin; they all went to the cider press and drank, except myself. On returning to the house, Hark went to the door with an axe, for the purpose of breaking it open, as we knew we were strong enough to murder the family, if they were awaked by the noise; but reflecting that it might create an alarm in the neighborhood, we determined to enter the house secretly, and murder them whilst sleeping. Hark got a ladder and set it against the chimney, on which I ascended, and hoisting a window, entered and came down stairs, unbarred the door, and removed the guns from their places. It was then observed that I must spill the first blood. On which, armed with a hatchet, and accompanied by Will, I entered my master's chamber, it being dark, I could not give a death blow, the hatchet glanced from his head, he sprang from the bed and called his wife, it was his last word, Will laid him dead, with a blow of his axe, and Mrs. Travis shared the same fate, as she lay in bed. The murder of this family, five in number, was the work of a moment, not one of them awoke; there was a little infant sleeping in a cradle, that was forgotten, until we had left the house and gone some distance, when Henry and Will returned and killed it; we got here, four guns that would shoot, and several old muskets, with a pound or two of powder. We remained some time at the barn, where we paraded; I formed them in a line as soldiers, and after carrying them through all the manoeuvres I was master of marched them off to Mr. Salathul Francis', about six hundred yards distant. Sam and Will went to the door and knocked. Mr. Francis asked who was there, Sam replied it was him, and he had a letter for him, on which he got up and came to the door; they immediately seized him, and dragging him out a little from the door, he was dispatched by repeated blows on the head; there was no other white person in the family. We started from there for Mrs. Reese's, maintaining the most perfect silence on our march, where finding the door unlocked, we entered, and murdered Mrs. Reese in her bed, while sleeping; her son awoke, but it was only to sleep the sleep of death, he had only time to say who is that, and he was no more. From Mrs. Reese's we went to Mrs. Turner's, a mile distant, which we reached about sunrise, on Monday morning. Henry, Austin, and Sam, went to the still, where, finding Mr. Peebles, Austin shot him, and the rest of us went to the house; as we approached, the family discovered us, and shut the door. Vain hope! Will, with one stroke of his axe, opened it, and we entered and found Mrs. Turner and Mrs. Newsome in the middle of a room, almost frightened to death. Will immediately killed Mrs. Turner, with one blow of his axe. I took Mrs. Newsome by the hand, and with the sword I had when I was apprehended, I struck her several blows over the head, but not being able to kill her, as the sword was dull. Will turning around and discovering it, despatched her also. A general destruction of property and search for money and ammunition, always succeded the murders. By this time my company amounted to fifteen, and nine men mounted, who

started for Mrs. Whitehead's, (the other six were to go
through a by way to Mr. Bryant's, and rejoin us at Mrs.
Whitehead's,) as we approached the house we discovered
Mr. Richard Whitehead standing in the cotton patch, near
the lane fence; we called him over into the lane, and Will,
the executioner, was near at hand, with his fatal axe, to
send him to an untimely grave. As we pushed on to the
house, I discovered some one run round the garden, and
thinking it was some of the white family, I pursued them,
but finding it was a servant girl belonging to the house, I
returned to commence the work of death, but they whom I
left, had not been idle; all the family were already murdered, but Mrs. Whitehead and her daughter Margaret. As
I came round to the door I saw Will pulling Mrs. Whitehead out of the house, and at the step he nearly severed her
head from her body, with his broad axe. Miss Margaret,
when I discovered her, had concealed herself in the corner,
formed by the projection of cellar cap from the house; on
my approach she fled, but was soon overtaken, and after
repeated blows with a sword, I killed her by a blow on the
head, with a fence rail. By this time, the six who had gone by
Mr. Bryant's, rejoined us, and informed me they had done
the work of death assigned them. We again divided, part
going to Mr. Richard Porter's, and from thence to Nathaniel
Francis', the others to Mr. Howell Harris', and Mr. T. Doyles.
On my reaching Mr. Porter's, he had escaped with his family.
I understood there, that the alarm had already spread, and
I immediately returned to bring up those sent to Mr. Doyles,
and Mr. Howell Harris'; the party I left going on to Mr.
Francis', having told them I would join them in that neighborhood. I met these sent to Mr. Doyles' and Mr. Harris'
returning, having met Mr. Doyle on the road and killed him;
and learning from some who joined them, that Mr. Harris
was from home, I immediately pursued the course taken by
the party gone on before; but knowing they would complete
the work of death and pillage, at Mr. Francis' before I could

get there, I went to Mr. Peter Edwards', expecting to find
them there, but they had been here also. I then went to Mr.
John T. Barrow's, they had been here and murdered him. I
pursued on their track to Capt. Newit Harris', where I found
the greater part mounted, and ready to start; the men now
amounting to about forty, shouted and hurraed as I rode up,
some were in the yard, loading their guns, others drinking.
They said Captain Harris and his family had escaped, the
property in the house they destroyed, robbing him of money
and other valuables. I ordered them to mount and march
instantly, this was about nine or ten o'clock, Monday morning. I proceeded to Mr. Levi Waller's, two or three miles
distant. I took my station in the rear, and as it was my object
to carry terror and devastation wherever we went, I placed
fifteen or twenty of the best armed and most relied on, in
front, who generally approached the houses as fast as their
horses could run; this was for two purposes, to prevent escape and strike terror to the inhabitants—on this account I
never got to the houses, after leaving Mrs. Whitehead's, until
the murders were committed, except in one case. I sometimes
got in sight in time to see the work of death completed,
viewed the mangled bodies as they lay, in silent satisfaction,
and immediately started in quest of other victims—Having
murdered Mrs. Waller and ten children, we started for Mr.
William Williams'—having killed him and two little boys that
were there; while engaged in this, Mrs. Williams fled and got
some distance from the house, but she was pursued, overtaken, and compelled to get up behind one of the company,
who brought her back, and after showing her the mangled
body of her lifeless husband, she was told to get down and
lay by his side, where she was shot dead. I then started for
Mr. Jacob Williams, where the family were murdered—Here
he found a young man named Drury, who had come on business with Mr. Williams—he was pursued, overtaken and shot.
Mrs. Vaughan was the next place we visited—and after
murdering the family here, I determined on starting for

Jerusalem—Our number amounted now to fifty or sixty, all mounted and armed with guns, axes, swords and clubs—On reaching Mr. James W. Parker's gate, immediately on the road leading to Jerusalem, and about three miles distant, it was proposed to me to call there, but I objected, as I knew he was gone to Jerusalem, and my object was to reach there as soon as possible; but some of the men having relations at Mr. Parker's it was agreed that they might call and get his people. I remained at the gate on the road, with seven or eight; the others going across the field to the house, about half a mile off. After waiting some time for them, I became impatient, and started to the house for them, and on our return we were met by a party of white when, who had pursued our blood-stained track, and who had fired on those at the gate, and dispersed them, which I knew nothing of, not having been at that time rejoined by any of them—Immediately on discovering the whites, I ordered my men to halt and form, as they appeared to be alarmed—The white men, eighteen in number, approached us in about one hundred yards, when one of them fired, (this was against the positive orders of Captain Alexander P. Peete, who commanded, and who had directed the men to reserve their fire until within thirty paces)—And I discovered about half of them retreating, I then ordered my men to fire and rush on them; the few remaining stood their ground until we approached within fifty yards, when they fired and retreated. We pursued and overtook some of them who we thought we left dead; (they were not killed) after pursuing them about two hundred yards, and rising a little hill, I discovered they were met by another party, and had halted, and were reloading their guns, (this was a small party from Jerusalem who knew the negroes were in the field, and had just tied their horses to await their return to the road, knowing that Mr. Parker and family were in Jerusalem, but knew nothing of the party that had gone in with Captain Peete; on hearing the firing they immediately rushed to the spot and arrived just in time to arrest the progress of these barbarous villians, and save the lives of their friends and fellow citizens). Thinking that those who retreated first, and the party who fired on us at fifty or sixty yards distant, had all fallen back to meet others with ammunition. As I saw them reloading their guns, and more coming up than I saw at first, and several of my bravest men being wounded, the others became panick struck and squandered over the field; the white men pursued and fired on us several times. Hark had his horse shot under him, and I caught another for him as it was running by me; five or six of my men were wounded, but none left on the field; finding myself defeated here I instantly determined to go through a private way, and cross the Nottoway river at the Cypress Bridge, three miles below Jerusalem, and attack that place in the rear, as I expected they would look for me on the other road, and I had a great desire to get there to procure arms and ammunition. After going a short distance in this private way, accompanied by about twenty men, I overtook two or three who told me the others were dispersed in every direction. After trying in vain to collect a sufficient force to proceed to Jerusalem, I determined to return, as I was sure they would make back to their old neighborhood, where they would rejoin me, make new recruits, and come down again. On my way back, I called at Mrs. Thomas's, Mrs. Spencer's, and several other places, the white families having fled, we found no more victims to gratify our thirst for blood, we stopped at Maj. Ridley's quarter for the night, and being joined by four of his men, with the recruits made since my defeat, we mustered now about forty strong. After placing out sentinels, I laid down to sleep, but was quickly roused by a great racket; starting up, I found some mounted, and others in great confusion; one of the sentinels having given the alarm that we were about to be attacked, I ordered some to ride round and reconnoitre, and on their return the others being more alarmed, not knowing who they were, fled in different ways, so that I was reduced to about twenty again; with this I determined to attempt to recruit, and proceed on to rally in the neighborhood, I had left. Dr. Blunt's was the nearest house, which we reached just before day; on riding up the yard, Hark fired a gun. We expected Dr. Blunt and his family were at Maj. Ridley's, as I knew there was a company of men there; the gun was fired to ascertain if any of the family were at home; we were immediately fired upon and retreated, leaving several of my men. I do not know what became of them, as I never saw them afterwards. Pursuing our course back and coming in sight of Captain Harris', where we had been the day before, we discovered a party of white men at the house, on which all deserted me but two, (Jacob and Nat), we concealed ourselves in the woods until near night, when I sent them in search of Henry, Sam, Nelson, and Hark, and directed them to rally all they could, at the place we had had our dinner the Sunday before, where they would find me, and I accordingly returned there as soon as it was dark and remained until Wednesday evening, when discovering white men riding around the place as though they were looking for some one, and none of my men joining me, I concluded Jacob and Nat had been taken, and compelled to betray me. On this I gave up all hope for the present; and on Thursday night after having supplied myself with provisions from Mr. Travis's, I scratched a hole under a pile of fence rails in a field, where I concealed myself for six weeks, never leaving my hiding place but for a few minutes in the dead of night to get water which was very near; thinking by this time I could venture out, I began to go about in the night and eaves drop the houses in the neighborhood; pursuing this course for about a fortnight and gathering little or no intelligence, afraid of speaking to any human being, and returning every morning to my cave before the dawn of day. I know not how long I might have led this life, if accident had not betrayed me, a dog in the neighborhood passing by my hiding place one night while I was out, was attracted by some meat I had in my cave, and crawled in and stole it, and was coming out just as I returned. A few nights after, two negroes having started to go hunting with the same dog, and passed that way, the dog came again to the place, and having just gone out to walk about, discovered me and barked, on which thinking myself discovered, I spoke to them to beg concealment. On making myself known they fled from me. Knowing then they would betray me, I immediately left my hiding place, and was pursued almost incessantly until I was taken a fortnight afterwards by Mr. Benjamin Phipps, in a little hole I had dug out with my sword, for the purpose of concealment, under the top of a fallen tree. On Mr. Phipps' discovering the place of my concealment, he cocked his gun and aimed at me. I requested him not to shoot and I would give up, upon which he demanded my sword. I delivered it to him, and he brought me to prison. During the time I was pursued, I had many hair breadth escapes, which your time will not permit you to relate. I am here loaded with chains, and willing to suffer the fate that awaits me.

I here proceeded to make some inquiries of him, after assuring him of the certain death that awaited him, and that concealment would only bring destruction on the innocent as well as guilty, of his own color, if he knew of any extensive or concerted plan. His answer was, I do not. When I questioned him as to the insurrection in North Carolina happening about the same time, he denied any knowledge of it; and when I looked him in the face as though I would search his inmost thoughts, he replied, "I see sir, you doubt my word; but can you not think the same ideas, and strange appearances about this time in the heaven's might prompt others, as well as myself, to this undertaking." I now had much conversation with and asked him many questions, having forborne to do so previously, except in the cases noted in parenthesis; but during his statement, I had, unnoticed by him, taken notes as to some particular circumstances, and having the advantage of his statement before me in writing, on the evening of the third day that I had been with him, I began a cross examination, and found his statement corroborated

by every circumstance coming within my own knowledge or
the confessions of others who had been either killed or executed, and whom he had not seen nor had any knowledge
since 22d of August last, he expressed himself fully satisfied
as to the impracticability of his attempt. It has been said
he was ignorant and cowardly, and that his object was to
murder and rob for the purpose of obtaining money to make
his escape. It is notorious, that he was never known to have
a dollar in his life; to swear an oath, or drink a drop of spirits.
As to his ignorance, he certainly never had the advantages of
education, but he can read and write, (it was taught him by
his parents,) and for natural intelligence and quickness of
apprehension, is surpassed by few men I have ever seen. As
to his being a coward, his reason as given for not resisting
Mr. Phipps, shews the decision of his character. When he
saw Mr. Phipps present his gun, he said he knew it was impossible for him to escape as the woods were full of men; he
therefore thought it was better to surrender, and trust to
fortune for his escape. He is a complete fanatic, or plays his
part most admirably. On other subjects he possesses an uncommon share of intelligence, with a mind capable of attain-
ing any thing; but warped and perverted by the influence of
early impressions. He is below the ordinary stature, though
strong and active, having the true negro face, every feature
of which is strongly marked. I shall not attempt to describe
the effect of his narrative, as told and commented on by himself, in the condemned hole of the prison. The calm, deliberate composure with which he spoke of his late deeds and
intentions, the expression of his fiend-like face when excited
by enthusiasm, still bearing the stains of the blood of helpless
innocence about him; clothed with rags and covered with
chains; yet daring to raise his manacled hands to heaven,
with a spirit soaring above the attributes of man; I looked
on him and my blood curdled in my veins.

I will not shock the feelings of humanity, nor wound
afresh the bosoms of the disconsolate sufferers in this un-

paralleled and inhuman massacre, by detailing the deeds of
their fiend-like barbarity. There were two or three who were
in the power of these wretches, had they known it, and
who escaped in the most providential manner. There were
two whom they thought they left dead on the field at Mr.
Parker's, but who were only stunned by the blows of their
guns, as they did not take time to re-load when they charged
on them. The escape of a little girl who went to school at
Mr. Waller's, and where the children were collecting for
that purpose, excited general sympathy. As their teacher had
not arrived, they were at play in the yard, and seeing the
negroes approach, she ran up on a dirt chimney, (such as
are common to log houses,) and remained there unnoticed
during the massacre of the eleven that were killed at this
place. She remained on her hiding place till just before
the arrival of a party, who were in pursuit of the murderers,
when she came down and fled to a swamp, where, a mere
child as she was, with the horrors of the late scene before
her, she lay concealed until the next day, when seeing a
party go up to the house, she came up, and on being asked
how she escaped, replied with the utmost simplicity, "The
Lord helped her." She was taken up behind a gentleman of
the party, and returned to the arms of her weeping mother.
Miss Whitehead concealed herself between the bed and the
mat that supported it, while they murdered her sister in the
same room, without discovering her. She was afterwards car-
ried off, and concealed for protection by a slave of the family,
who gave evidence against several of them on their trial. Mrs.
Nathaniel Francis, while concealed in a closet heard their
blows, and the shrieks of the victims of these ruthless savages; they then entered the closet, where she was concealed,
and went out without discovering her. While in this hiding
place, she heard two of her women in a quarrel about the
division of her clothes. Mr. John T. Baron, discovering them
approaching his house, told his wife to make her escape, and
scorning to fly, fell fighting on his own threshold. After firing
his rifle, he discharged his gun at them, and then broke it

over the villain who first approached him, but he was over-powered, and slain. His bravery, however, saved from the hands of these monsters, his lovely and amiable wife, who will long lament a husband so deserving of her love. As directed by him, she attempted to escape through the garden, when she was caught and held by one of her servant girls, but another coming to her rescue, she fled to the woods, and concealed herself. Few indeed, were those who escaped their work of death. But fortunate for society, the hand of retributive justice has overtaken them; and not one that was known to be concerned has escaped.

The Commonwealth,	Charged with making insurrection,
vs.	and plotting to take away the lives of
Nat Turner	divers free white persons,

&c. on the 22d of August, 1831.

The court composed of ———, having met for the trial of Nat Turner, the prisoner was brought in and arraigned, and upon his arraignment pleaded *Not guilty;* saying to his counsel, that he did not feel so.

On the part of the Commonwealth, Levi Waller was introduced, who being sworn, deposed as follows: (*agreeably to Nat's own Confession.*) Col. Trezvant[*] was then introduced, who being sworn, narrated Nat's Confession to him, as follows: (*his Confession as given to Mr. Gray.*) The prisoner introduced no evidence, and the case was submitted without argument to the court, who having found him guilty, Jeremiah Cobb, Esq. Chairman, pronounced the sentence of the court, in the following words: "Nat Turner! Stand up. Have you any thing to say why sentence of death should not be pronounced against you?

Ans. I have not. I have made a full confession to Mr. Gray, and I have nothing more to say.

Attend then to the sentence of the Court. You have been arraigned and tried before this court, and convicted of one

[*] The committing Magistrate.

of the highest crimes in our criminal code. You have been convicted of plotting in cold blood, the indiscriminate destruction of men, of helpless women, and of infant children. The evidence before us leaves not a shadow of doubt, but that your hands were often imbrued in the blood of the innocent; and your own confession tells us that they were stained with the blood of a master; in your own language, "too indulgent." Could I stop here, your crime would be sufficiently aggravated. But the original contriver of a plan, deep and deadly, one that never can be effected, you managed so far to put it into execution, as to deprive us of many of our most valuable citizens; and this was done when they were asleep, and defenseless; under circumstances shocking to humanity. And while upon this part of the subject, I cannot but call your attention to the poor misguided wretches who have gone before you. They are not few in number— they were your bosom associates; and the blood of all cries aloud, and calls upon you, as the author of their misfortune. Yes! You forced them unprepared, from Time to Eternity. Borne down by this load of guilt, your only justification is, that you were led away by fanaticism. If this be true, from my soul I pity you; and while you have my sympathies, I am, nevertheless called upon to pass the sentence of the court. The time between this and your execution, will necessarily be very short; and your only hope must be in another world. The judgment of the court is, that you be taken hence to the jail from whence you came, thence to the place of execution, and on Friday next, between the hours of 10 A.M. and 2 P.M. be hung by the neck until you are dead! dead! dead! and may the Lord have mercy upon your soul.

A list of persons murdered in the Insurrection, on the 21st and 22nd of August, 1831.

Joseph Travers and wife and three children, Mrs. Elizabeth Turner, Hartwell Prebles, Sarah Newsome, Mrs. P.

Reese and son William, Trajan Doyle, Henry Bryant and wife and child, and wife's mother, Mrs. Catharine White-head, son Richard and four daughters and grand-child, Salathiel Francis, Nathaniel Francis' overseer and two children, John T. Barrow, George Vaughan, Mrs. Levi Waller and ten children, William Williams, wife and two boys, Mrs. Caswell Worrell and child, Mrs. Rebecca Vaughan, Ann Eliza Vaughan, and son Arthur, Mrs. John K. Williams and child, Mrs. Jacob Williams and three children, and Edwin Drury—amounting to fifty-five.

A List of Negroes brought before the Court of Southampton, with their owners' names, and sentence.

Name	Owner	Sentence
Daniel,	Richard Porter,	Convicted.
Moses,	J. T. Barrow,	do.
Tom,	Caty Whitehead,	Discharged.
Jack and Andrew,	Caty Whitehead	Con. and transported
Jacob,	Geo. H. Charlton,	Disch'd without trial.
Isaac,	Ditto,	Convi. and transported.
Jack,	Everett Bryant,	Discharged.
Nathan,	Benj. Blunt's estate,	Convicted.
Nathan, Tom, and Davy, (boys,)	Nathaniel Francis,	Convicted and transported
Davy,	Elizabeth Turner,	Convicted.
Curtis,	Thomas Ridley,	Do.
Stephen,	Do.	Do.
Hardy and Isham,	Benjamin Edwards,	Convicted and transp'd.
Sam,	Nathaniel Francis,	Convicted.
Hark,	Joseph Travis' estate.	Do.
Moses, (a boy,)	Do.	Do. and transported.
Davy,	Levi Waller,	Convicted.
Nelson,	Jacob Williams,	Do.
Nat,	Edm'd Turner's estate	Do.
Dred,	Wm. Reese's estate	Do.
Arnold, Artist, (free)	Nathaniel Francis,	Do.
Sam,		Discharged.
Ferry and Archer,	J. W. Parker,	Acquitted.
Jim,	J. W. Parker,	Disch'd. without trial.
Bob,	William Vaughan,	Acquitted.
Davy,	Temperance Parker,	Do.
Daniel,	Joseph Parker,	
Thomas Haithcock, (free,)	Solomon D. Parker	Disch'd without trial.
Joe,		Sent on for further trial.
Lucy,	John C. Turner,	Convicted.
Matt,	John T. Barrow,	Do.
Jim,	Thomas Ridley,	Acquitted.
Exum Artes, (free,)	Richard Porter,	Do.
Joe,		Sent on for further trial.
Bury Newsome, (free,)	Richard P. Briggs,	Disch'd without trial.
Stephen,		Sent on for further trial.
Jim and Isaac,	James Bell,	Acquitted.
Preston,	Samuel Champion,	Convicted and trans'd.
Frank,	Hannah Williamson	Acquitted.
Jack and Shadrach,	Solomon D. Parker	Convi'd and transp'd.
Nelson,	Nathaniel Simmons	Acquitted.
Sam,	Benj. Blunt's estate,	Do.
Archer,	Peter Edwards,	Convicted.
Isham Turner, (free,)	Arthur G. Reese,	Acquitted.
Nat Turner,	Putnam Moore, dec'd.	Sent on for further trial. Convicted.

CONTRIBUTORS

John Henrik Clarke is professor emeritus of African world history of Hunter College, City University of New York. He was born in Union Springs, Alabama in 1915. His recent publications include *African People in World History, Africans at the Crossroads: Notes for an African World Revolution, My Life in Search of Africa*, and *Who Betrayed the African World Revolution?*

Lerone Bennett, Jr., is executive editor of *Ebony Magazine*. His poems, short stories, and articles have appeared in many publications. His books include *Before the Mayflower, The Negro Mood, What Manner of Man, Confrontation: Black and White*, and *The Shaping of Black America*, an analysis of African American history. He was born in Clarksdale, Mississippi in 1928. After graduating from Morehouse College, he worked for the *Atlanta World*.

Loyle Hairston is a freelance writer who has published widely. He is a member of the Harlem Writers Guild and contributor to two volumes of essays: *Harlem: A Community in Transition* and *Harlem, U.S.A.* He is now a retired postal supervisor.

Charles V. Hamilton is the Wayne S. Sayre Professor of Government at Columbia University. He is author of the *Black Preacher in America, The Bench and the Ballot: Southern Federal Judges and Black Voters, The Black Experience in American Politics*, and a recent biography, *Adam Clayton Powell, Jr.: A Biography of an American Dilemma*. He is coauthor with Stokely Carmichael (now Kwame Toure) of *Black Power*.

Vincent Harding is Professor of religion at the School of Religion, University of Denver. His books include *There is a River* and *Hope in History*. He is a founder of the Institute of the Black World in Atlanta, Georgia.

Ernest Kaiser was editor of the *Freedomway's Reader* forum before he retired. A highly respected bibliographer, his essays have been published widely in journals and collected volumes, such as *Harlem: A Community in Transition*.

John O. Killens was born in Macon, George in 1916 and was educated in the South and North. His career was launched with the highly successful first novel *Youngblood*. *And Then We Heard the Thunder*, his second novel, was based partly on his experiences in the South Pacific as a World War II soldier. *The Great Black Russian*, a biography of Alexander Pushkin, was his last work before he died in 1987.

Alvin Poussaint is professor of psychiatry, New England Medical Center Hospitals, Clinical Unit. An active participant in the Civil Rights Movement, his popular articles have been published in the *New York Times*, *Ebony Magazine*, and other publications.

Mike Thelwell is professor of English at the University of Massachusetts, Amherst. He is author of scholarly articles and is also a widely published freelance writer and civil rights activist.

John A. Williams, novelist and essayist, is professor of English and writing at Rutgers University. His novels include *Night Song, Sissie*, and *The Man Who Cried I Am*. He has also published the travel book *This Is My Country Too*.